PROGRAMMING TO BUILD DISCIPLES

A Strategy for Encouraging
Students toward Spiritual Growth

DUFFY ROBBINS

VICTOR BOOKS™
A DIVISION OF SCRIPTURE PRESS PUBLICATIONS INC.
USA CANADA ENGLAND

Unless otherwise noted, Scripture quotations are from *New American Standard Bible,* © the Lockman Foundation 1960, 1962, 1963, 1968, 1971, 1972, 1973, 1975, 1977. Other quotations are from the *Holy Bible, New International Version* (NIV), © 1973, 1978, 1984, International Bible Society. Used by permission of Zondervan Bible Publishers; and the *Revised Standard Version of the Bible* (RSV), © 1946, 1952, 1971, 1973.

Library of Congress Catalog Card Number: 86-63164
ISBN: 0-89693-573-6

© 1987, SP Publications, Inc. All rights reserved.
Printed in the United States of America.

CONTENTS

Foreword		5
Chapter One	Programming to Build Disciples	7
Chapter Two	The Problem of Attacking Richmond	13
Chapter Three	Turning a Vision into a Program	19
Chapter Four	A Blueprint for Youth Ministry	25
Chapter Five	Bringing It All Together	31
Chapter Six	Programming for Higher Levels of Commitment	41
Chapter Seven	Onward Bound: A Program of Personal Growth and Discipleship	51
Chapter Eight	Personal Reflection	59
Bibliography		60

Acknowledgments

This short book has actually been several years in the making. Through those years, there have been a number of people who have had a hand in its creation.

For that reason, I wish to thank J.L. and Patt Williams of the New Directions Evangelistic Association who originally built into me and my wife a vision for the ministry of multiplication.

Thanks to Robert Coleman, Trinity Evangelical Divinity School, whose writings sparked in me a desire to follow "The Master Plan of Evangelism."

I'm especially grateful to the youth groups of Barrington Baptist Church, Barrington, Rhode Island and the United Methodist Church of Wilmore, Kentucky. These folks gave me the great privilege of sharing their lives, and it was in that adventure that I had the chance to impart and sharpen my ministry of disciple-making. It was my experiences with these young disciples, and others like them, that built into me a strong commitment to minister with students.

My sincere thanks goes to our office staff, particularly Kim Feeser and Mary Noel Keough, without whom this manuscript would still be lost somewhere in the word processor. The Lord only knows what it's like to be secretary to both Tony Campolo and Duffy Robbins, and yet these women bear this cross with grace and humor. God bless them.

■ Duffy Robbins

FOREWORD

A marksman firing with no target in sight will surely hit it. The tragedy is that all the shooting can be mistaken for accomplishment.

This is obvious in ministry with young people. Far too many workers expend energy running hither and yon, frantically trying to keep a program going, without any clear sense of direction. Activity may be equated with fulfillment.

The question has to be asked, "Where are we going?" Only then can we ascertain if what we are doing is worth the effort.

Duffy Robbins in this book honestly faces this basic issue. With keen insight and biblical realism, he sees beyond the necessity of getting attendance at youth meetings and comes to grips with the compelling mandate of Christ to make disciples. Recognizing that kids are at different stages of development, he analyzes their levels of receptivity to the Gospel claims and proposes ways to meet them. Through it all, the focus is on people, not mere programs.

The author writes out of years of experience as a youth leader in churches, and now as a college professor. There is a ring of credibility in his perception. Both as a practitioner and as a scholar he knows where ministry should lead, and in getting there he does not lose the reader in a smog of words. More to the point, he makes sense. This is the kind of book that gets the rubber down to the road. Those who have struggled with the task of equipping young men and women for fruitful Christian living will find it right on target.

> Dr. Robert E. Coleman, Director
> School of World Mission and Evangelism
> Trinity Evangelical Divinity School

To Maggie, my wife, friend, and co-minister, and to Erin and Katie, the two precious little girls that God has given us as our number-one ministry of discipleship.

CHAPTER ONE

Programming to Build Disciples

■ Maybe you've heard the story about the man and his wife riding down a busy freeway. Her complaints and grumbling come out at almost the same fast speed he is driving. After about twenty minutes, twenty-five miles, and twenty-nine insults, this gentleman has had it. He loses it all and screams, "Will you stop nagging me? OK! You're right! We're lost! But, you gotta admit, we're making great time!"

Unfortunately, that is characteristic of the way a lot of folks approach youth ministry. We give more attention to distance and speed than to ultimate destination. It's no wonder that a lot of our youth programs are running out of gas. We're spending our money, our people, and our time trying to build good youth ministries, while in most cases we've given almost no thought to the two key questions: Where are we now? and Where do we want to go?

There are several different approaches to the "Lost-on-the-Freeway Syndrome." Probably the most common response is the one we see in the hapless, heavy-footed husband mentioned in the opening paragraph. Most of us are too busy to be bothered with questions about destination. "We've got some kids meeting in the church basement on Sunday nights. They're pretty regular. Something must be right. Let's not rock the boat!" As long as our programs are on the move, we would rather not be bothered with questions like: "Where are they moving to?"

A second type of response commonly seen in our youth ministries is this sort: "You're right, I think we are lost. Let's just keep on driving until we see something that will get us back on track." So we spend more money, more time, and more people hoping we will stumble into the "right" direction, searching through each new promotional mailing, resource packet, or youth magazine article hoping that we will find just the right idea, just the right route, to get us back on the highway of "successful" youth ministry. Never mind that we've still no sense of destination or even our present location. More movement, more programs, and more money will surely get us back on track.

A third response that is all too common in our youth ministries is the kind exhibited by this statement: "Well, we can't be lost. Look at all the cars on this same freeway. If it's working for them, it ought to work for us. Let's just keep going." We don't stop to ask ourselves if we really want to go to the same destination as the others using this route. And, of course, there are many routes to the same destination, but the right route is the route that begins where you are!

Probably, the most typical response of our local churches to the "Lost-on-the-Freeway Syndrome" is represented by a fourth statement: "You're right. We are lost. We don't know where we're going. We've got to do something drastic! Let's buy a new car!" So many churches who sense that their programs are aimless and ineffective decide for some reason that their best response to the situation is to either build a new building or shop around for a new program—a new idea book, a new curriculum, or a new magazine resource. But, if a church is "lost on the freeway," buying a new car isn't going to solve the problem.

Only One Solution

There is only one response that makes much sense when you are lost on the freeway. Only one response can keep us from driving aimlessly for an unknown, undetermined destination until we either run out of road, run out of gas, run out of drivers, or run out of kids who are willing to ride with us! We start by pulling over, turning off the engine, and taking a good long look at the map! This book is about you and your youth ministry. It is about honest evaluation of where your group is and where it should be heading. And, it is about how you can get there.

If I had been reading this book in my early years of youth ministry, I would have read through that last paragraph and decided right away that the first part of this book could be ignored. "That's just philosophy, and what counts when you're working with kids is not what you think; it's what you do." Confident that my two years of vast experience had helped to avoid wasting time I could be spending with kids, I would plunge straight ahead to the "ideas" section of the book. Looking for new exits and new routes, I wouldn't have taken the necessary time to ask myself where my program was and where was it headed.

There are a lot of reasons why most youth ministries take the same approach:

(1) Evaluation takes time. That's a commodity that most youth workers don't have. "I don't have time to talk theory, man. I'm just trying to survive through Sunday night."

(2) Evaluation is inconvenient. It may mean that we have to make some changes, and that always shakes up church people.

(3) The embarrassing thing about defining a target is that we may finally discover that after all this time, we've been missing the mark. Personally, as a self-confessed William Tell, with a seminary degree and four years of youth ministry under my belt, I was not eager to hear that.

On the Other Hand...

I chuckled the first time a colleague in youth ministry said to me, "There's only one thing worse than driving a van load of junior-high kids to a bowling alley, staying there for two hours, and then driving them back to the church for an all-night lock-in (everybody knows better than to call them "*sleep*-overs"!) and that is doing all of that once a month, and then going home tired on Saturday morning, sleeping through a potential Saturday with your family, and then waking up Saturday afternoon without really being sure *why* you had done it, or *what* you had actually accomplished."

I stopped chuckling after about two years of youth ministry.

On Friday nights, when I said good-bye to my wife and left my kids at home so I could spend the evening with somebody else's kids, I couldn't avoid asking myself what I was accomplishing with this activity. Where would it take me? I didn't chuckle very much when one of my ministry team members resigned because he "just wasn't motivated" to spend so much time with the kids when he couldn't see we were going anywhere.

Don't get me wrong. I loved the youth in our group. We had some super times and our group was getting bigger. The congregation was impressed, but deep down I knew: I was making great time, but I had no sense of where I was going.

"Without a Vision..."

Forced to reevaluate our program, I took a careful look at where we were. I surveyed our kids on a variety of issues. I read books, talked to colleagues, and prayed. And I began to realize something that has changed my ministry: If I hoped to work with kids for very long, I would have to be sustained by a vision that was bigger than Friday night's rock-a-thon, Sunday night's pizza party, and Tuesday night's skate-down (our kids were "holy rollers"). I needed a vision that was worth my life, my enthusiasm, and my energy. Without that vision, like some of my team members, and so many of my *ex*-youth minister friends, I knew I couldn't go the long haul.

Proverbs 29:18 reads, "Where there is no vision, the people perish" (KJV).

Another translation renders this verse: "Where there is no vision, the people are unrestrained" (NASB). By "pulling over" in my own ministry, I had a chance to go back to the map. There, in the Scriptures, I found a mandate for ministry that has given my years of youth work purpose, focus, and genuine vitality. Having a biblically defined destination, I was able to develop programs that would route my students and leaders in a direction that would help us reach our goals. In the pages that follow, I'm going to share that vision. It's really not a new idea. But I hope this book will provide some new strategies for making that vision a reality in your youth program. Maybe it will keep some of us from being lost on the freeway. I *can't* promise you'll *ever* develop a taste for junior-high lock-ins!

■

WHAT ABOUT YOU?

Use this sheet for personal evaluation.

1. How would you define the "destination" (goals) of your youth ministry?

   Group unity/sense of "groupness"
   Heart for missions/the lost
   Lordship of Christ.

   How would the majority of your students define the destination of your ministry? The parents connected with your ministry? Your pastor? Do they know or understand your vision?

   Group unity - not much beyond this.

2. What aspects of your youth ministry make it difficult to reach your destination?

   Small group size/
   my lack of motivation

3. Which of the five possible responses to the "Lost-on-the-Freeway Syndrome" represents your own response in the past? Why?

   I want to do what others are doing and being successful at.

4. What steps can you take to begin reevaluating your ministry? (You may want to jot down some key questions to ask your students and colleagues.)

   Pray
   I've already asked staff & students - no one knows

5. What are some ways you can share your youth ministry vision with others who need to understand it?

   Parents meeting
   Share w/ students/staff

CHAPTER TWO

The Problem of Attacking Richmond

■ Lorne Sanny, President of the Navigators, recounts that back during the Civil War, there was a bit of confusion in the high command of the Union Army. It seems that President Lincoln could not dissuade his generals from launching an attack on Richmond, Virginia. Why the generals had this obsession for capturing Richmond is unclear (though it can be a tough town if you don't know anybody), but Lincoln's generals persisted. Finally, Lincoln challenged his strategists with this observation: The Confederate Army is not in Richmond! (Author's Note: That may be why they wanted to attack Richmond!) Lincoln asked, "What good will it do to capture the city? You will only gain geography. Gentlemen, our purpose is to win a war" (from "Laborers: the Navigators' Mission," Navigators *Daily Walk* Devotional Guide).

One of our problems in youth ministry is that we are constantly fighting the wrong battles, winning the wrong objectives, and consequently, losing the war. The mind-set of the church is too often geared toward gaining geography that will not ultimately help us to win the war. That's why it's so important for those of us in youth ministry to define a specific objective, a specific goal, a vision that guides our strategy.

A Fresh Look at the Map

The best way to determine that vision, the only real solution to the Lost-on-the-Freeway Syndrome is to pull over and take a fresh look at the map. The Scripture gives us a clear sense of what our destination, our objective, our vision ought to be. Let's take a quick look at three separate passages.

Matthew 28:19

In Matthew 28:19 Jesus' followers were commanded, *"Go and make disciples* of all nations, baptizing them in the name of the Father and of the Son and of the Holy Spirit, and teaching them to obey everything I have commanded you" (italics added). Over the years the church has called this command "the Great Commission." In reality, as one preacher noted, it should be called "the Great Omission"! Like much of the church, we in youth ministry have forgotten that our number-one priority is not to build big youth groups or flashy youth programs. We are called to build people. Anything less than that is an attack on Richmond! It might gain us some geography, but it won't win the war.

Ephesians 4:11-14

In Ephesians 4:11-14 we are given a clear mandate for the church at large, a mandate that has very real implications for those of us in youth ministry. Basically, our call is to *"equip saints for the work of ministry*, for the building up of the body of Christ, until we all attain to the unity of the faith and of the knowledge of the Son of God" (Eph. 4:12-13, RSV).

But this passage in Ephesians 4 is even more appropriate as we continue in verses 13 and 14. Here is a special challenge for those of us who work with "teenage saints" (which may sound like a contradiction to some people!) to lead these saints into "mature personhood, to the measure of the stature of the fullness of Christ; so that they may no longer be children, tossed to and fro and carried about with every wind of doctrine, by the cunning of men, by their craftiness in deceitful wiles" (Eph. 4:13-14, RSV). What a perfect description of the task we face in guiding teenagers through the moral maze of questions and confusion surrounding adolescence, building them up in the faith so that they can see through the propaganda of the world and help them to grow into mature people who have senses of identity and conviction.

2 Timothy 2:2

Here is instruction given by Paul to Timothy his "young son in the faith," instruction that when viewed from the perspective of youth ministry gives us yet another confirmation of the call to build people equipped for ministry. Paul writes, "The things you have heard me say in the presence of many witnesses entrust to reliable men who will also be qualified to teach others"

CHAIN OF MULTIPLICATION
adapted from Waylon Moore's *Multiplying Disciples*

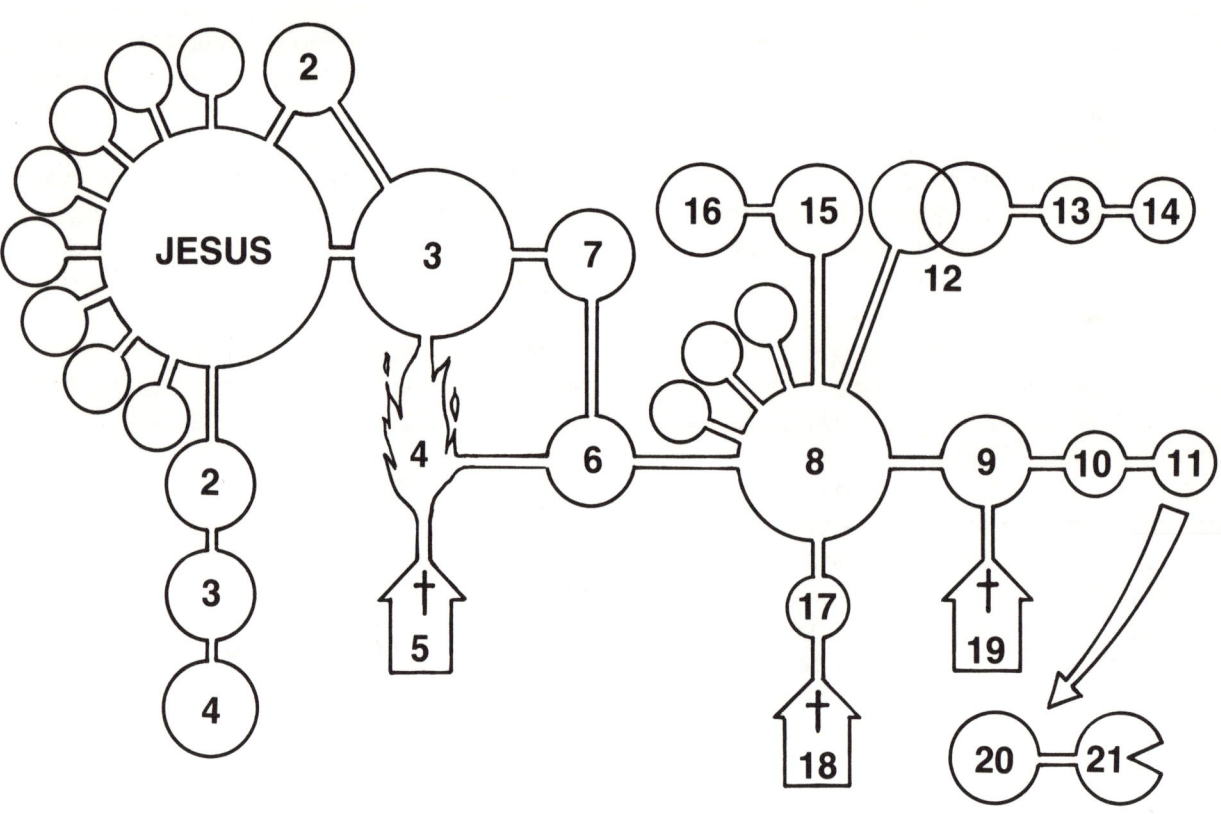

KEY

2. Andrew
3. Simon Peter
4. Pentecost
5. Antioch
6. Barnabas
7. John Mark
8. Paul
9. Timothy
10. Faithful men
11. Others also
12. Priscilla and Aquila
13. Apollos
14. Jews
15. Luke
16. Theophilus
17. Titus
18. Crete
19. Ephesus
20. Bald-headed youth minister
21. Today's teen

(2 Tim. 2:2, NIV). A quick glance at this verse will show four different generations of spiritual reproduction:

- First generation: Paul
- Second generation: Timothy
- Third generation: Reliable men
- Fourth generation: Others

Few verses of Scripture hint at the profound impact one person can have by simply equipping a young person (Timothy, in this case) for the work of ministry.

Waylon Moore, in an excellent book, *Multiplying Disciples* (NavPress), depicts this principle of multiplication even more dramatically. Notice the diagram which appears on page 14.

Obviously, this kind of ministry takes time. It takes commitment. And it requires a vision that extends beyond the question of how many youth show up for this week's bowling party. But, in a nutshell, that is where the map tells us we need to be going. We need to be captured by that vision. Our volunteer coworkers need to be called to that vision. And our parents and kids need to know that this is why our youth ministry exists. (I can still remember one of my youth group kids saying that he heard me refer to 2 Timothy 2:2 so often that he was just going to start calling it "Tutti-Tutu"!) Other objectives may be easier to attack. Other destinations may be more popular, and the routes to reach them may be exciting and fun, but this, at the bottom line, is where we are called to move.

Ah, Yes, but What Is a "Disciple"?

Pure and simple: The goal of youth ministry is building disciples. But what does a teenage disciple look like? Are they people who have short hair? How do they act on dates? Or do they date at all? Can a male disciple have pierced ears? (Trick question. Of course not!) We have a lot of different ideas about discipleship. Some would say that a teenage disciple of Christ is a young person with short hair and middle-class values who doesn't "smoke, drink, cuss, or chew, or go out with the girls that do." Others use the word "disciple" to describe everybody from a committed Springsteen fan to a follower of the Rajneesh! Jot down in the space below your general definition of a Christian disciple.

Person totally in love w/ and following Jesus daily.

"Disciple" was Christ's favorite word for those whose lives were linked with His. The Greek word, *mathétes,* is used 269 times in the Gospels and Acts. Essentially, it means "one who is taught," a "trained one." There are two sets of passages listed below. The first set includes three verses in which Jesus gives a clear statement about how He characterizes discipleship. The second set of verses is a passage in which Jesus three times makes a statement about discipleship using the formula: "If _____, he *cannot* be My disciple." Read through these passages to sharpen your own sense of what it means to be a disciple, and write additions to your definition.

Set #1: John 8:31: *A disciple holds to the teachings of Jesus*

John 13:34-35: *Disciples love each other as Jesus commanded.*

John 15:1-8: *A disciple remains connected to Jesus as his/her source*

Set #2: Luke 14:25-33: *1. You must hate everything before X/carry cross Count the cost of following Jesus*

Fruit comes from being in the vine, not striving

Drawing from Scripture, there seem to be at least three essential characteristics of someone who is a disciple of Jesus Christ:

(1) the person is growing in conformity to Christ;
(2) the person is fruitful in efforts to bring others to Christ;
(3) the person is working to conserve that fruit by doing adequate follow-up, the result of which will be another Christlike, fruitful disciple who is able to reproduce himself/herself.

To really make that vision a reality, a destination we can intentionally aim for, we need to be prepared to translate these characteristics of discipleship into the teenage life experience.

For example, we need to think through with our youth how a teenager lives differently on a day-to-day basis if that teenager is a disciple, a follower of Jesus Christ. It is not enough to give vague guidelines here. Until we have thought through this question in a very practical sense, we will not know what kinds of habits, traits, and disciplines to build into students. The target must be marked clearly enough so that one can know if one has "hit" or "missed," but loosely enough so that our description of "a disciple" is not legalistic or culturally bound.

Far too many youth ministers leave the notion of following Jesus, and being His disciple, on such spiritual terms that teens are unwilling to volunteer because either they don't understand what is expected of them, or they volunteer too easily because they don't understand the stakes. We must be practical here. How helpful is it to tell a teenager that he "cannot be a disciple" unless he is willing to "hate his father and mother, his wife and children, his brothers and sisters—yes, even his own life"? (Luke 14:25-33) That might sound too good to be true to some teenagers I know! We need to help kids translate these characteristics into everyday experience. That means that our focus is going to have to be less on building programs, and more on building people.

Profile of a Christian Teenager: A Brainstorming Exercise

Dean is a senior in high school. He plays on the football team, is well-liked around school, and a die-hard "Ultimate Frisbee" player. Dean is also a disciple of Jesus Christ. Finish your work in this chapter by brainstorming what Dean might "look" like. Think through various areas of his life that are going to be different because of his Christian commitment. If Dean were to graduate from your youth group this spring, what are some of the key qualities, values, patterns that you would hope to have built into his life? Record your thoughts in the space below.

■

He would be involved in service
Witnessing to his friends
He wouldn't participate in locker room discussions and would say why.
He probably would have few close friends.

WHAT ABOUT YOU?

Use this sheet for personal evaluation.

1. List the "battles" you fight in your ministry.

   Motivation
   attendance
   activities

2. Which of these only help you gain geography?

3. Which are most likely to help you win the war?

4. Rate your own ministry on progress toward the biblical objective of building disciples.

   Weak   **Strong**

   1   2   ③   4   5   6   7

Why did you give yourself that rating?

I've been so focused on building the group that I haven't worked at building disciples.

CHAPTER THREE

Turning a Vision into a Program

■ No one has ever accused me of being an art critic, but I was intrigued by an article I came across in the *Philadelphia Inquirer* (October 7, 1984) about an eccentric artist who was scheduled to exhibit at the Philadelphia Museum of Art. In the early days, before Jonathan Borofsky launched his career as a "power artist," he spent day after day in his New York loft apartment doing nothing but counting. That's right. One-two-three-four, and so on. Borofsky explains that it was an act of near desperation, an attempt to try to bring some order into his life.

"Like a mantra . . . I'd bring all my thinking down to one thought," Borofsky explains, "reducing the noise in my head to one simple, clear, poetic, mathematical noise." As time went on, Borofsky became more ambitious in his counting, filling sheets of graph paper with numbers, one number to a square, 200 to 300 numbers to a page, with numbers on both sides of the paper, changing pen colors occasionally to add the artistic touch. (And you thought junior high kids were weird!)

As any youth worker surely knows, all creative people face adversities and skepticism. The Borofsky counting project was no different. At one point, during an argument with his girlfriend, sheets with the first 20,000 numbers were destroyed—four months of work down the tubes! On another occasion, a stroke of creative genius led him to begin affixing minus signs to the numbers, a whim that took him all the way back to minus 12,000 before he regained his forward motion. The most interesting part of this portrait of Borofsky was one comment made by the artist himself. Reflecting on the moment that he had passed a million after two years of counting, he said, "I thought maybe something would happen in my mind, but nothing. I just kept counting."

What is most remarkable about that statement, other than Borofsky's own apparent surprise at this discovery, is that it is a perfect illustration of the kind of frustration and disappointment that comes about when the sole focus of one's ministry is numbers—higher attendance, bigger crowds, constant counting. The tragedy is that this is precisely where so many of us in youth ministry place our bets. Like David (2 Sam. 24:10), we number the troops, hoping for a sense that certainly God is blessing this enterprise, thinking, like Borofsky, that at some point something will happen, "but nothing." And even more tragic, like Borofsky, a lot of youth ministries "just keep going."

There is a certain attraction to the kind of program that draws big crowds and features week after week of fun, high-visibility events. Once the machinery is in place, these programs are usually easier to maintain. As Borofsky puts it, you reduce it all down to "one simple, clear, poetic, mathematical noise." I hope I'm not a stick-in-the-mud, but I don't think that sort of approach makes very good art or very good ministry.

Pat Hurley (*Penetrating the Magic Bubble*, Victor, pp. 12-17) characterizes this approach to ministry as Program-oriented. Its basic goal is to build a strong program. He contrasts that approach with one that is Person-oriented. The differences between these two approaches are real and will make a difference in the nuts-and-bolts ways we program our ministries. Consider the chart on the next page.

Program-oriented Ministry	Person-oriented Ministry
(1) GOAL is a good program: high visibility, functions smoothly, easy to promote.	GOAL is building people into disciples, "saints equipped for work of ministry."
(2) STARTS with ideas: Youth or volunteer receives mailing or hears of "wild, new idea"; decides to try it with group and see what happens.	STARTS with needs of kids involved; all programming strategies and ideas filtered through the question: How will it help us get students from where they are to deeper commitment?
(3) SUCCESS judged by attendance: the more kids in the program, the better; lots of counting!	SUCCESS judged by individuals who have been involved with the ministry: Where are they now? How solid is their commitment? Are they "equipped saints"?
(4) PRODUCES large numbers initially (if it's done well) and involves lots of people. Well-liked by kids; tends to play to "wants" rather than needs. Impresses congregation.	PRODUCES long-term results. May start small and be less impressive in the short run. Usually builds in more "staying power."
(5) PREDICTABLE: Once a "working" system is established that seems to please everybody, no need to make changes.	FLEXIBLE: A program based on needs will change as needs change; may even necessitate changing a popular program to better meet objectives.

Building a Person-oriented Program

If you've ever dealt with a travel agent, you know that there are two pieces of information essential for that agent to properly service your business. Number one: that agent needs to know where you're going. Number two: that agent needs to know where you're coming from. It sounds odd, but a good trip-planner works backward, starting with the destination, then pinpointing the point of departure, and then, as a last step, choosing the route.

That is the way to plan for person-oriented ministry. It's the program-oriented approach which begins by choosing an idea, or an activity, a route, and *then* choosing a destination—obviously, not a good way to plan if you have a set destination in mind.

This book has already tried to define a biblical destination for youth ministry. Our goal is to build disciples. But, how does one go about defining that "point of departure"? Person-oriented ministry begins when we try to inventory the needs of the youth involved in the ministry. Who are the kids currently involved within the ministry's sphere of influence? Where are those kids right now—spiritually, emotionally, physically, and socially?

Sound youth ministry begins with a thorough assessment of the present group, a step often neglected at great expense in time and energy. It's amazing how many youth ministry ideas are planned and programmed for groups that don't exist! Group profiles can be collected by preparing surveys that the youth respond to, or through one-on-one conversations, or by taking an evening to allow group members to collectively evaluate themselves. The key here is to listen. Keep the proverbial ear to the ground. Probe. Watch. Talk with parents, volunteer leaders, and church officials. Above all, don't choose a route until you've determined your point of departure.

Larry Richards, in his classic work, *Youth Ministry: Its Renewal in the Local Church* (Zondervan), has identified three broad categories of involvement that can be helpful as criteria for evaluating a youth group: Bible, life, and body. The following diagram might be a tool you can use to find your group "on the map."

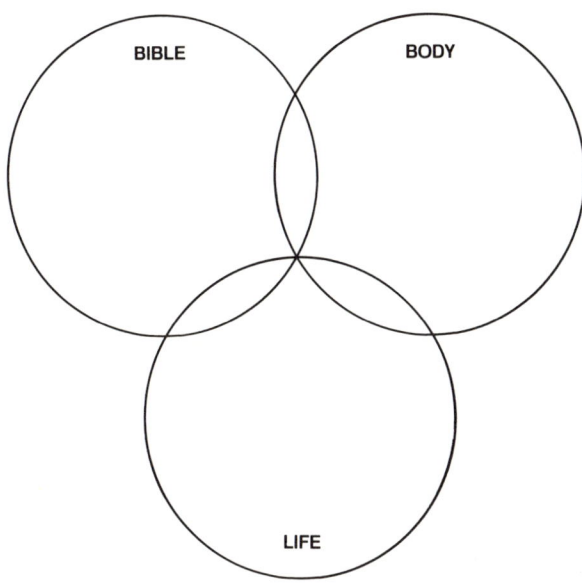

RICHARDS' DIAGRAM

BIBLE: We begin by recognizing that if we hope to lead our students into maturity, through adolescence with its cacophony of lies, temptations, pressures, and uncertainties, we must help them understand the Word of Truth. We must acquaint our youth with the Bible, its doctrines, its instructions, its main themes. We need also to enable our kids to begin to discover these truths on their own so that as they confront the pressures of adulthood, they needn't hide behind old stories that "somebody told me," but can draw from a tough faith that can survive their world.

LIFE: Bible knowledge alone is not enough, though. God's truth is of little value to us if it isn't processed and worked out in the daily affairs of life. The second area of need that youth ministry must address is the task of building disciples who can take "Truth" into their marketplace, into their schools, on their dates, into their interpersonal relationships, into their evaluations of media messages through video, TV, movies, and music. We need to test our ministries to see if we are helping our teens evaluate their living habits in light of Scripture.

This is also the point at which we assess the "world-awareness" of our students. In what sense are they taking responsibility for bringing healing to their world at hand, as well as to the world at large? Responsible discipleship means taking seriously the mission implications of the Gospel. Christian teenagers may be strong on "Bible," know all the right verses, and speak fluent "Christianese." But they still need to be challenged that New Testament Christianity confronts them with the needs of hurting people around them.

BODY: Even a consistent Christian lifestyle falls short of the biblical picture of discipleship, though. We haven't really gotten to our destination until we have confronted our students with the responsibilities they have as members of the body of Christ. Please, let's think of this as more than formal confirmation and membership! It is that, to be sure. But, it is also encouraging students into relationships with commitment—affirming each other, holding each other accountable, encouraging each other, stimulating one another to love and good works (Heb. 10:24-25). In a teenage culture that celebrates using people for self-fulfillment, and is more often characterized by comments that "cut" than by comments that heal, those kinds of relationships come through practical instruction and genuine opportunities for community.

Having a group evaluation of the three key areas can provide some healthy eye-opening, and it might be a good exercise for a volunteer team, a parent's youth ministry support group, a deacon board, or the youth themselves. There are lots of options for how this can be done. One possible format involves the survey which follows on page 23.

Note: Take some time as you discuss the survey to explain each area of involvement. It's a good opportunity to remind group members why the group exists!

SAMPLE SURVEY

"Are We There Yet?"

You remember that question! Anytime you're on a trip, that's the question you ask your dad every five minutes to help him relax! He kind of looks at the surroundings, checks out the map, swallows hard, and says, "No, I think we're going to have to head in this direction for a while."

Well, that's what this survey is about. We know we haven't "arrived" yet, but we do want to make sure we're moving in the right direction. So, we need your input about where we need to go next, what we might have passed too quickly, or where you think we got lost or sidetracked.

In each of the circles below, jot down your thoughts about your youth group using each of these categories of reference. Look at the surroundings, check out the map (the Bible) if you want to, swallow hard, and let us know what you think.

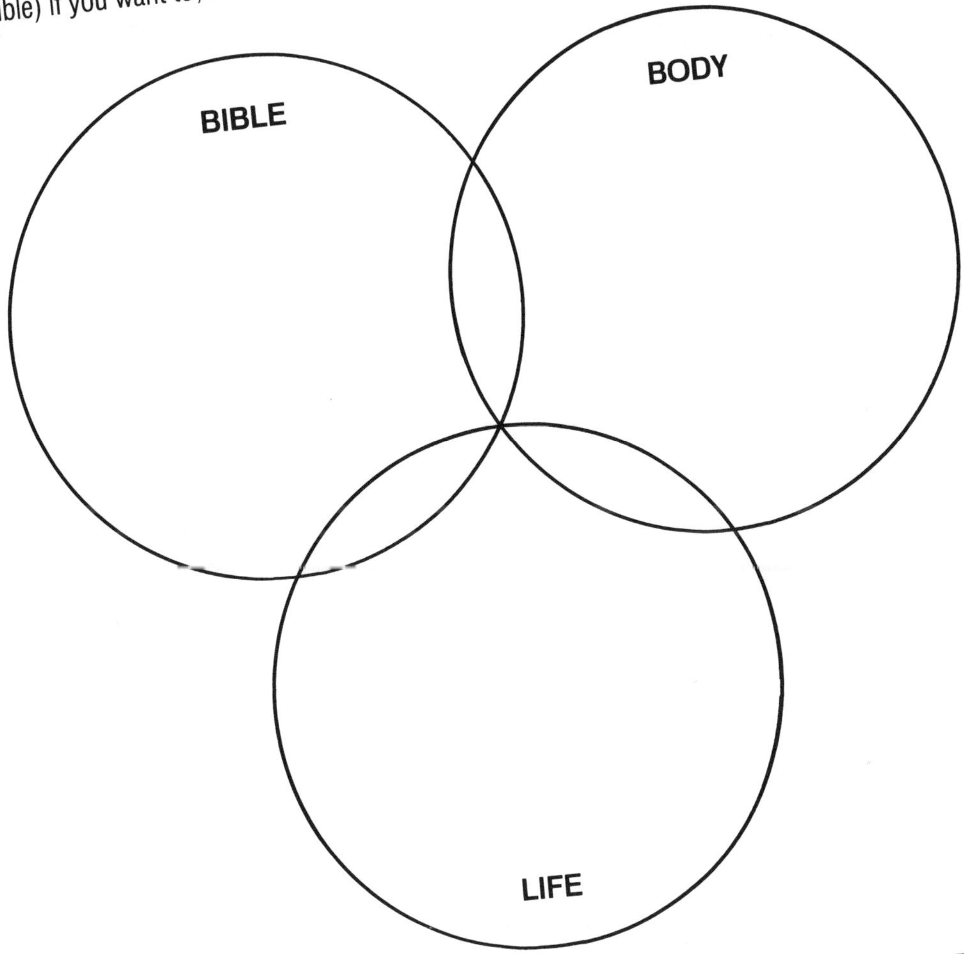

BIBLE

BODY

LIFE

23

WHAT ABOUT YOU?

Use this sheet for personal evaluation.

1. Place a mark on the continuum showing where your ministry would fall.

Program-oriented ☐☐☐☐☐☐☐☐☐☐☐■☐☐☐☐☐ Person-oriented

2. How important are "numbers" in your ministry—

	Very Important						Not at All Important
■ *To you?*	1	2	3	4	(5)	6	7
■ *To parents?*	1	2	3	(4)	5	6	7
■ *To church leadership?*	1	2	3	(4)	5	6	7
■ *To youth?*	1	2	(3)	4	5	6	7

3. Make a list of questions you would include in a survey of your group members:

I would like to teach the 3 areas and then discuss where they feel we are weak or strong.

CHAPTER FOUR

A Blueprint for Youth Ministry

Several years ago, the *Providence Journal* ran a story under the headline "Big Names to Have Dirty Linen Aired." The article detailed the results of a study done by the state of Massachusetts examining cases in which state funds may have been poorly used. Ironically, the study itself, a two-year project of a special commission, cost the state $1.5 million. The results were *almost* amusing (unless, of course, you're a Massachusetts taxpayer!). By the time the report came out, there were a lot of red-faced public servants running for cover.

Among literally hundreds of case studies were these highlights (*Providence Journal,* "Massachusetts—Big Names to Have Dirty Linen Aired," Loring Swaim):

- *"The Boston State College 13-story tower, one of the largest buildings ever built by the Commonwealth.* Its top five floors, intended as a library, have been shut off since 1976 because the designer failed to include any centralized security checkpoints. Accordingly, the five floors have been heated, air-conditioned, and unused for four years. The college's auditorium is so constructed that one cannot see the stage from the balcony.
- *"The Haverhill (Mass.) parking deck.* It is so poorly designed it can only be demolished and rebuilt." Apparently, part of the problem here was in fitting some cars up the ramp of this magnificent structure!
- *"The multimillion dollar University of Massachusetts power plant.* It was built too far from the buildings it services—and never used."

The reason these state-financed gaffs are only "*almost* amusing" is because it is tragically reflective of what goes on consistently in youth ministries all across the country today! We continue to spend astronomical amounts of time, money, and energy on programs and structures so that we can say, "It's the largest ever built," but half the time the finished product cannot even be used. We are building power plants that don't deliver power—and that's not very funny!

Immediately following some very serious statements about discipleship, Jesus said, "For which one of you, when he wants to build a tower, does not first sit down and calculate the cost, to see if he has enough to complete it? Otherwise, when he has laid a foundation, and is not able to finish, all who observe it begin to ridicule him, saying, 'This man began to build and was not able to finish' " (Luke 14:28-30).

To build the kind of youth ministry program that will accomplish the purpose for which it was built, serious consideration needs to be given to the "blueprint." I've talked with a lot of youth ministers over the last several years who use as the blueprint for their programs a pyramid-type concept. (While I would like to believe that the pyramid shape authenticates the biblical, Mideastern roots of this model, it's not really clear who was the first to develop the idea.) It has several variations, but the diagram on the next page gives the basic picture.

Essentially, what this diagram does for us is help us evaluate and develop our youth ministry programs by showing us the kinds of students our programs are addressed to. Looking at the diagram, we need to think of each of the levels of the pyramid as representing students at varying levels of Christian commitment. The higher the level on the pyramid, the higher the level of

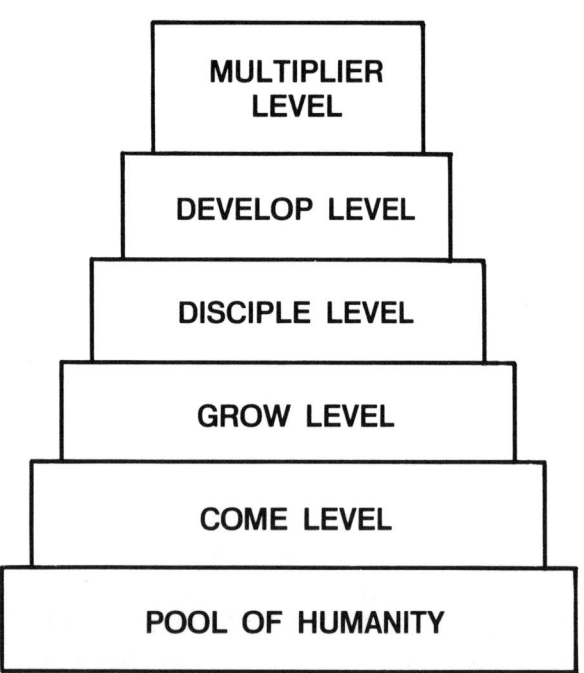

commitment. Let's look briefly at each level of the pyramid.

Pool of Humanity

This level of the pyramid represents the teenage population in general, the teenagers within your geographical sphere of influence. Your group, in fact, may not have any influence on these students at the present time. The vast majority of these kids may not even know you or your ministry exist. But you know about them, and by God's grace and power you want to reach them with the Gospel.

For example, my current Pool of Humanity while here at Eastern College in St. Davids, Pennsylvania includes at least three to four public high schools within a five-mile radius. Because of the socio-economic makeup of St. Davids and the surrounding suburbs of western Philadelphia (known as the Main Line), there are also probably twice that many private prep schools.

Now, for someone to do person-oriented youth ministry in this area, these are simply some facts that must be reckoned with. This information, and other social and religious data about these youth, would help someone design a program uniquely suited to this area. And that's important because you don't have to be in youth ministry very long to discover that what works great in Tacoma or Tallahassee may bomb in Philadelphia (and vice versa). So, for a program to begin right, it is wise to begin by assessing your unique pool of humanity.

Come Level

Billy is one of those kids who never shows up for prayer breakfast or Sunday School, and always seems to have unavoidable conflicts that prevent his helping out with fund-raisers and work projects. Spiritually, he ranks somewhere between "plant life" and "lower primate," and whenever you "pass the hat" with Billy in the crowd, you're always just a little relieved to get your hat back!

The picture isn't completely negative, though. There are two areas for which Bill has shown tremendous interest and zeal: one is food, and the other is girls. Whenever a youth group activity allows for a large selection of either, you can count on Billy to be there! Billy doesn't make any pretense about it. He does not have any real commitment to Christ, but he does have a strong commitment to having a good time.

There are kids like Billy in any youth ministry I've ever been around. Theirs is a *Come Level* commitment. Their only commitment to the group is to come when the group is doing something they like—something fun or entertaining.

It's not uncommon to hear youth workers complain about kids like Billy. After all, we're called to build disciples and we "can't afford to waste time with some student who isn't willing to get serious about his walk with Christ." But that complaint raises some important questions. To be sure, our goal is to build students into multipliers, and that takes a certain degree of spiritual drive.

But, let's be honest and shrewd enough to admit that (a) Most teenagers on the outside of our ministries just are not mysteriously born with that degree of spiritual vitality; and (b) a majority of the students on the inside of our groups aren't there either. If we only program for the spiritual heavyweights, we are going to touch the lives of very few kids.

And (c) even more important, we need to remember that today's multiplier was yesterday's (or yesteryear's) "disinterested" Come Level kid. By the same token, today's Come Level teens might become tomorrow's disciples if we can somehow bring them within the influence of our ministry so that we can give them love, training, and attention.

Grow Level

Students at the *Grow Level* are students within our program environment who are willing to submit themselves to spiritual growth. These are the teens who take part in a youth activity, even if it involves them in some amount of Bible study or spiritual input. Essentially, that is the difference between kids at the Come Level and kids at the Grow Level.

Sally, a young woman with a Grow Level commitment, was not excited about the four Bible studies scheduled for the Winter Retreat Weekend, but she was willing to go along anyway. Her boyfriend, Sonny, who had a love for downhill skiing and an acute allergy to spiritual matters, decided not to sign up for the retreat. He reasoned that four Bible studies was too high a price to pay even if it meant being close to his favorite sport and his favorite girlfriend. His is a good example of Come Level commitment.

I am grateful for both students—for the chance to have some input into their lives. I am pleased that Sally is at least open enough to "take a chance" on the retreat. But, I also respect Sonny's fear of being uncomfortable with the spiritual activity that will be a part of the retreat. I can affirm both teens for where they are, while praying and working to take them both to deeper levels of commitment.

This is a good point to be reminded of two important realities.

(1) Willingness to grow is not the same thing as commitment to growth.

Kids at the Grow Level are not seeking spiritual growth on their own initiative. They will come to Bible study on Wednesday night, or take part in Sunday night meetings, but only because it requires little more than their passive involvement. We should not assume that a teenager at weekly Bible study is hungry for spiritual food and willing to take the initiative to get it.

That's a consideration to remember in preparing weekly Bible studies for youth group. That is not to say that we should short-change Bible

study time in favor of "fun and games." It is to say that we need to see part of our agenda as being evangelistic and that we should not assume students are walking into Bible study saying, "Fill my cup." Attention needs to be given to providing Bible study opportunities that incite student interest, invoke active participation, and equip students with the tools for taking responsibility for their own spiritual growth.

(2) Consistent attendance is not an indication of consistent commitment.

I didn't understand the Grow Level commitment early on in my ministry with students. I misinterpreted a student's strong commitment to me or to the program as being a strong commitment to Christ.

That was a delusion clearly exposed for me when one of my most active students graduated from high school, and from the youth group, went away to college, and almost immediately made an apparent, conscious decision to abandon any principles of Christian living. Obviously, it was a real disappointment to me, but it was also a real education.

It may be naiveté or just wishful thinking, but it's a common mistake of youth ministers to assume that just because kids are involved in spiritual activity, they are personally involved in spiritual growth. It's wonderful that kids are willing to submit themselves to spiritual growth, but let's not mistakenly assume that this means they will automatically, of their own initiative, develop a pattern of continued growth and fellowship following graduation.

Disciple Level

When a student in the youth group begins to take the initiative for his or her own spiritual growth, this student has matured to what might be described as a *Disciple Level* commitment. We've already examined the kinds of characteristics that one might expect to find in a teenager at this level of commitment (chapter 2). Suffice it to say that the key here is the word "discipline." A student at the Disciple Level is a student who is willing to discipline himself—to do personal Bible study on his own, memorize Scripture (even if it isn't a requirement for the choir tour), or personally seek to be a witness at school, at home, or wherever.

The role of the youth worker at this stage is to provide instruction and tools for students to pursue their own spiritual development. A teen may exhibit genuine willingness to study the Bible for himself, but that desire can burn out if the teen isn't given some personal help and guidance about how that kind of development happens.

Develop Level

As students begin to advance in spiritual growth, they will in time move into the next level of commitment. Teens at the *Develop Level* are students willing to take the initiative, not only for their own spiritual growth, but for the spiritual growth of others as well.

It's very important to mention here that the Develop Level of any lasting youth ministry will include both youth *and adults*. These youth and adults are people with whom the youth worker can begin to do a focused work of training and equipping for ministry. Without going into much detail about this training process, it might be helpful to simply remember two basic concepts:

(1) Training is a progressive work that begins with the instructor *modeling* the task, and eventually turning over responsibility for the task to the trainee.

(2) Ministry training should begin with physical responsibilities (e.g., arrange the chairs, line up transportation, plan a skit, set up the movie), and then expand to include spiritual responsibilities (lead the Bible study, share a devotion, give a testimony).

Very important to note here is that the Develop Level comes *after* the Disciple Level and not the reverse. I have seen the pyramid concept published by at least one source in which these two levels were given in the reverse order. In my estimation, that's a serious mistake.

We already have far too many youth and adults in church leadership who, perhaps unwittingly, have assumed responsibility for the spiritual growth of others, but have not demonstrated any willingness to take responsibility for their own spiritual growth. That is not the pattern we are given in 1 Timothy 3 and other passages where Paul writes about spiritual leadership.

This is a particularly easy trap to fall into in youth ministry because we are occasionally confronted with students and would-be volunteers who have all kinds of leadership ability, but all the spiritual depth of a Cabbage Patch doll. This is especially common with an elected youth council or youth advisory board since their makeup is usually determined more by popularity and status than by spiritual maturity. It is tempting to pass over the less charismatic student who shows genuine spiritual depth in favor of the one who is head cheerleader or star quarterback, but if we are talking about development of spiritual leadership, we had better remember that, "God sees not as man sees" (1 Sam. 16:7).

Multiplier Level

The final level of commitment is that point at which students begin to catch a vision for going back into their own junior high and high schools and starting the process over, reproducing it in the lives of their own friends or classmates. When we help move kids into this level of commitment, we are multiplying our own efforts in much the same way that Paul multiplied his by pouring himself into Timothy.

To be very realistic, it has been quite easy to move through these levels of commitment in only a few book pages. Unfortunately, the movement doesn't usually come that easily in real life ministry with kids. (How's that for understatement?)

One of my favorite illustrations of this process of growth draws from the world of the emperor penguin. While the parallels may not seem obvious at first (!) they are very real.

When the female emperor penguin has laid the eggs, she leaves the nest to fatten herself on fish from the frigid arctic waters. The remarkable fact is that at this point, the male emperor penguin steps in and gingerly places the newly laid egg on top of his feet, where he stands without moving, carefully balancing it there for the next two months until it hatches!

Ah, yes! If that is not a picture of youth ministry, I don't know what is. Here you have this newly hatched life, with only the promise, the potential for maturity. It cannot care for itself or survive without patient oversight. But, if we hang tough, stand strong, trust God, and wait, there will emerge yet another being who is capable of that same reproductive process.

WHAT ABOUT YOU?

Use this sheet for personal evaluation.

Think about the individual young people in your own group. Do any strong examples of Come, Grow, Disciple, and Develop Level kids come to mind? Choose one from each category and write a profile of each describing why and how he or she fits into that category:

Come

Grow

Most of our group falls into this catagory
Mandy,
Daniel
Maria
Ann
Leah

Disciple

Mindy
Kristin
Chris
Mike
Kate

Develop

CHAPTER FIVE

Bringing It All Together

■ After you've been in youth ministry for a while, you begin to grow intensely skeptical of models and blueprints. I suppose it's like shopping for a car: the design may be beautiful in the drawing room, the lines may be sleek and attractive in the showroom, but the ultimate question is, "How does it run?"

The best way to understand the pyramid illustrated in chapter 4, with its various levels of commitment, is to imagine the pyramid being turned upside down and taking on the shape of a funnel. (Turn this book upside down and try it. Surprise!) For the less mechanically inclined, study the diagram below. When you begin to visualize your ministry this way, you can do some careful evaluation of your youth program.

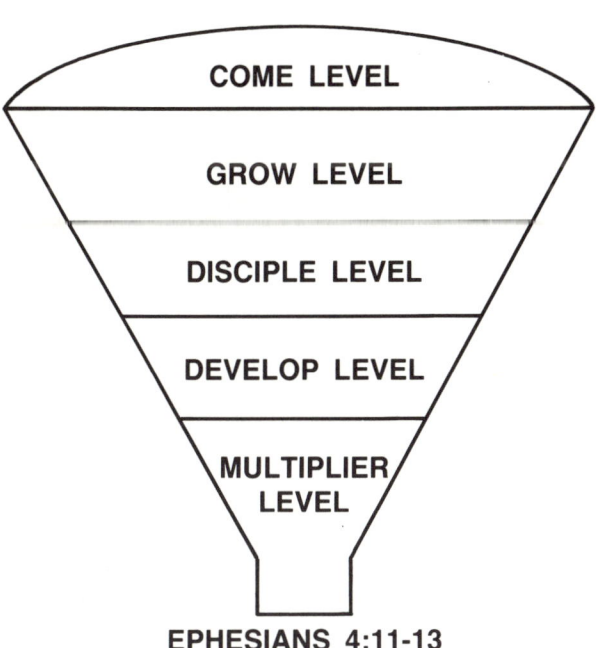

For a youth program to be well-rounded, accomplishing the purpose for which it was designed, there needs to be some type of formal or informal programming that will meet the needs of kids at each of these levels of commitment. There need to be Come Level programs, geared to the student who is "not into religion at all," and there need to be programs that will motivate the forward progress and growth of those at the Grow, Disciple, and Develop Levels.

The beauty of this kind of evaluation is that it helps you see where a particular youth program is overweight and where it's underweight, what kinds of students have been programmed for and, perhaps, what levels of commitment have been inadvertently ignored. This is where you make the hard decisions that will determine whether your current program fits the kind of blueprint that will yield the program and product you intend.

Some Important Considerations

When one sees the pyramid/funnel concept clearly, it becomes obvious that there are two important implications for youth ministry.

(1) *The Law of Spiritual Commitment*—We've seen it in our ministries for a long time, but we see it clearly here: *As commitment increases, attendance decreases.* This was true of Jesus' ministry and it will be true of ours. Five thousand people came out to get fed by Jesus (Matt. 14:14-21) but how many of those 5,000 followed Jesus into Jerusalem and Golgotha when opposition grew stronger and risks became greater?

I am amazed when youth workers question me with genuine sincerity saying, "I don't understand it. We get forty kids out to our swim party at the lake, but we only got fourteen at our Bible study Tuesday night." I want to smile and say, "Hey, welcome to the world! Kids like swimming better than they like studying the Bible!" Let's face that, understand it, and then move on.

What we do clearly need to understand is that when we judge a program by attendance, we may be using a very deceptive criterion. A Disciple Level program that is really helping you build stronger believers may not draw the crowds that a high visibility Come Level program draws, but, in reality, it may be a much more vital part of the youth ministry environment.

This is an important dynamic not only for youth workers to understand, but also parents, pastors, and youth committees. At first glance, it may not seem wise to put more money and time into a small group of people, when in terms of attendance, much greater payoff is seen elsewhere. But, that's where we need to see that these students and programs at the Disciple and Multiplier Levels are the "bread and butter" of our ministry. That doesn't mean that we shortchange the Come Level program. It does mean that so much of the time when we are putting a huge amount of energy into programs that bring in lots of kids, programs with high visibility and much excitement, we might be "capturing Richmond," but that alone won't help us to win the war.

(2) The Importance of the "Unspiritual"—In one congregation where I used to work as youth minister, there was one mother who always got on my case whenever we did an "unspiritual" activity like white-water rafting or playing Ultimate Frisbee. She considered it a total waste of time—certainly not what I was getting paid to do!

If this mother had understood the principle of the funnel, she could have understood, perhaps, that in the right program environment, even the "unspiritual" activities have very legitimate, spiritual goals. After all, the most spiritually intensive program in the world doesn't do anybody any good if students won't take part in it. It may make some parishioners feel good to know that "the youth are having their all-night prayer meeting instead of going to the Amy Grant concert." But, if there aren't any kids at the all-night prayer meeting, that *really is* a waste of time!

As a balance for the Law of Spiritual Commitment, we need to realize that we can't get students to be multipliers if we can't involve them in leadership development. And we can't get them involved at the Develop Level if we don't get them discipled. And we can't get them discipled if we can't get them interested in growth. And we can't get them to grow if we can't get them to come. And that might mean that the most spiritually strategic action I can take with some students is to take them away with me for a day of white-water rafting, building relationships, and breaking down defenses.

With these thoughts in mind, we're ready to move into the process of evaluation.

Evaluating a Youth Program: Three Stages
Stage one: Where are the kids?

The first stage in evaluating your current youth ministry is to get some idea of the kinds of students involved in your program. Either by yourself, or with the help of your adult volunteers, simply work through the roster of the group and, as closely as possible, try to place each individual at one of the five levels of commitment in the pyramid. Use the blank pyramid on the next page. If it's helpful, use symbols to indicate a "growth spurt," a renewed commitment, or even a current "mellowing" of spiritual fervor. For large groups, you may want to draw up a pyramid for each grade grouping.

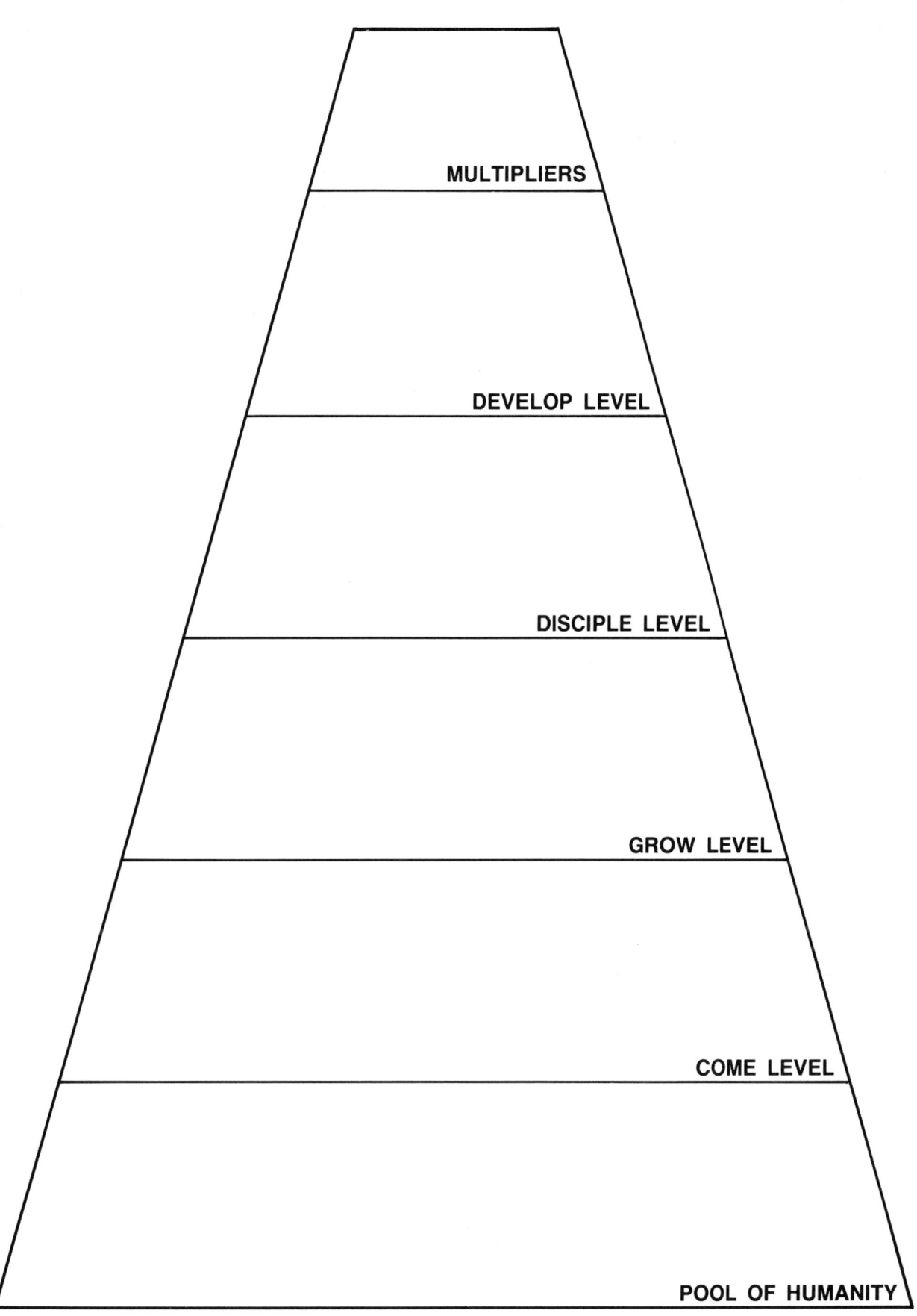

EXAMPLE: High School Group—First Church

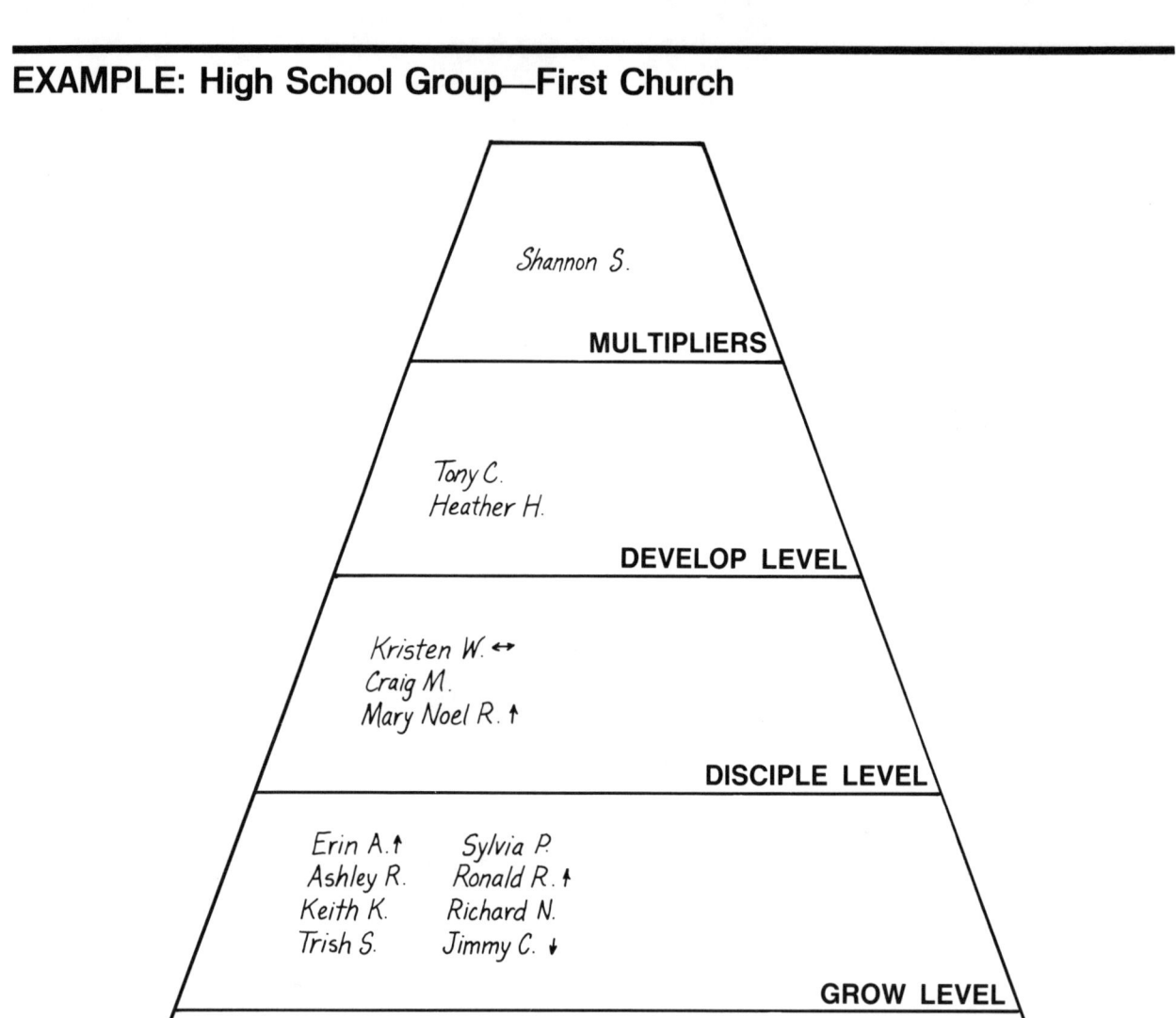

Stage two: Where is the program?

For the second phase of evaluation, the funnel diagram is more helpful. Using the blank funnel on the following page, do an inventory of your youth program. What kinds of programs do you have that would minister to students at the various levels of commitment? Are there any programs that seem to overlap more than one level of commitment? Are most of the programs geared to Come and Grow Level commitment? Where in the program do you feed and nurture kids at the deeper levels of commitment?

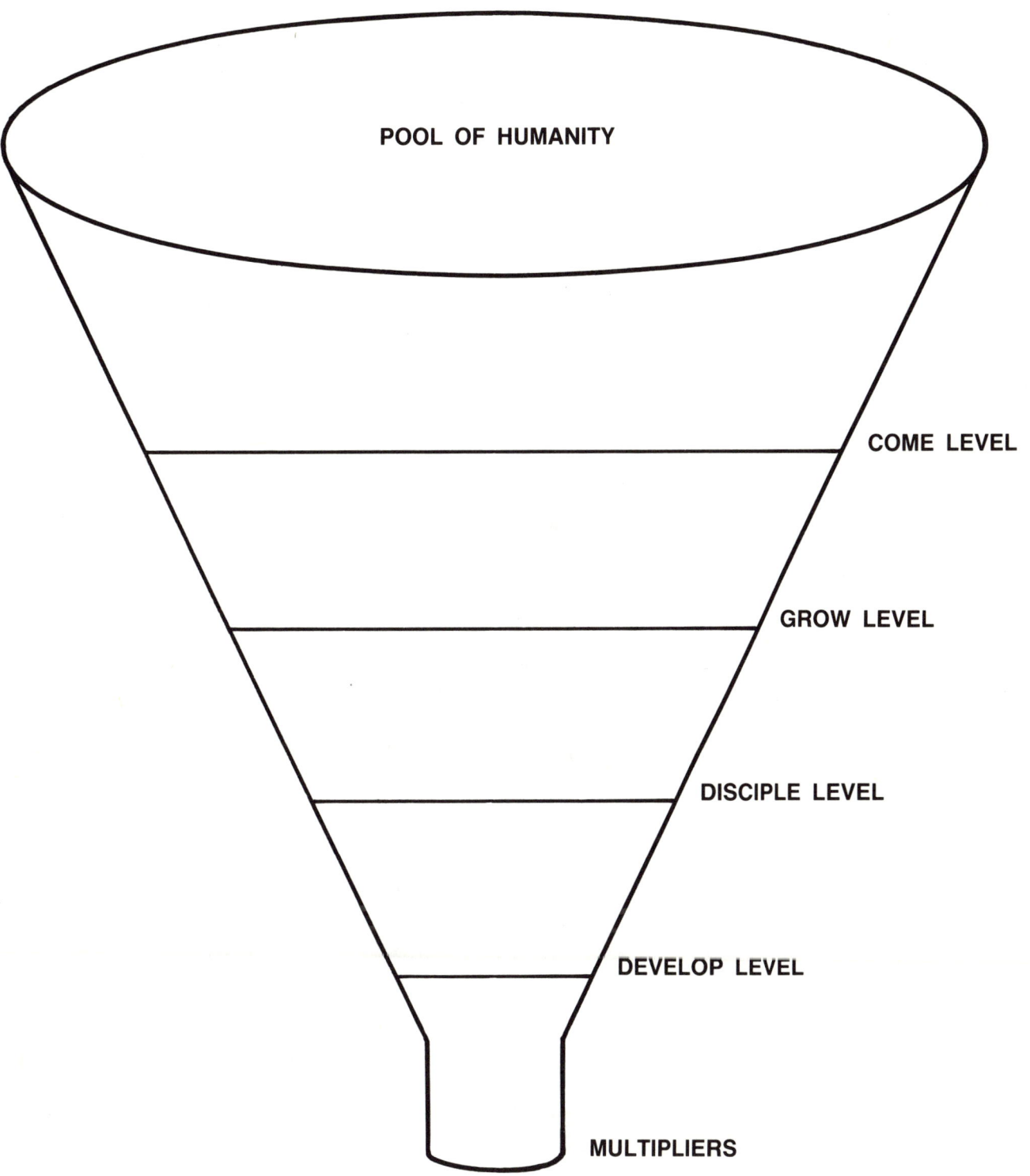

Programming to Build Disciples - Duffy Robbins
Victor Books, 1987

SAMPLE EVALUATION: High School Ministry—First Church

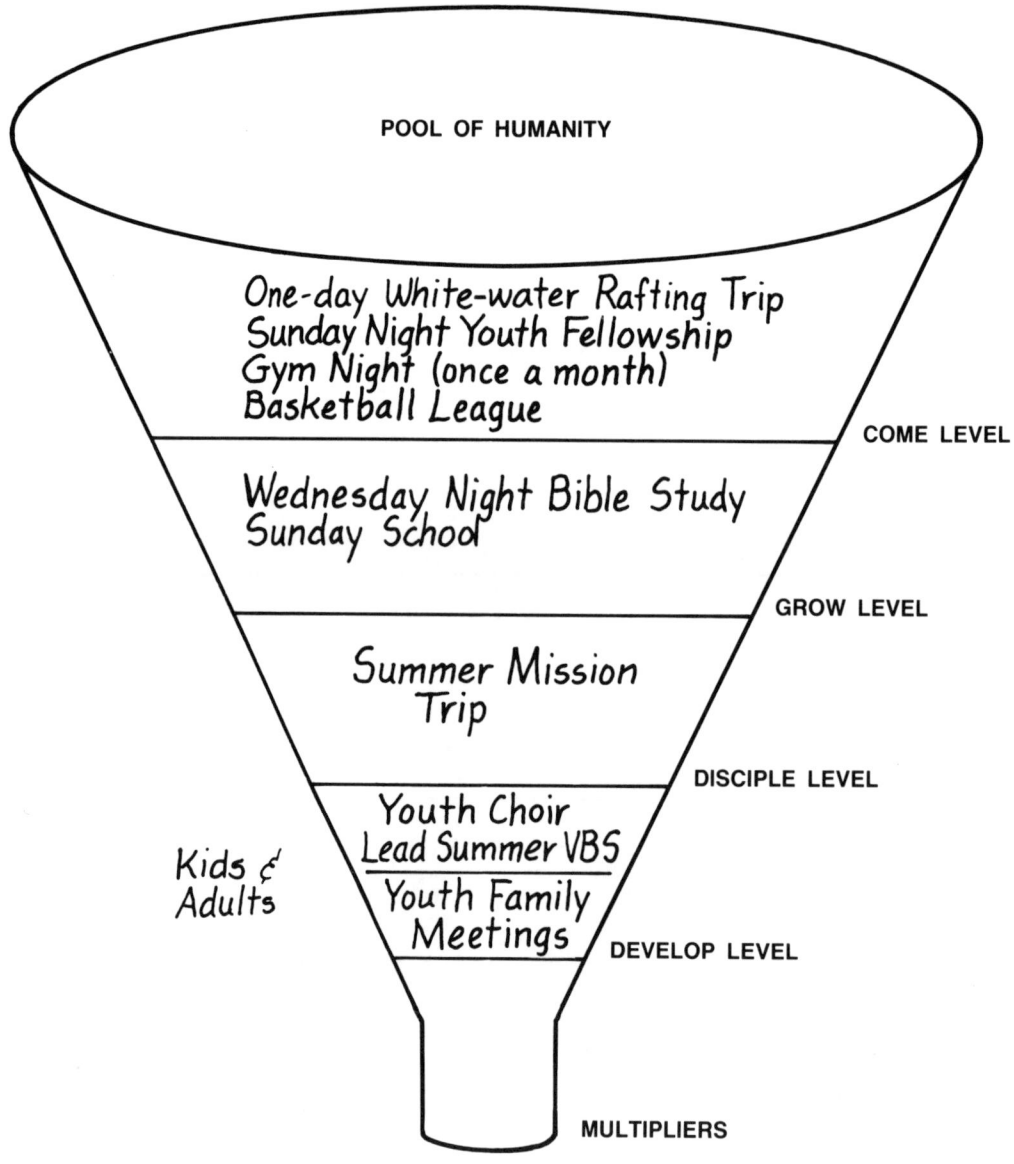

Stage three: "Does it run?"

With stage two complete, you are ready to do the serious work of deciding if this program you've built actually accomplishes the purpose for which it was designed. If we're honest, we may find along with that special Massachusetts commission that some of our "towers" can't be used and some of our "power plants" aren't delivering power.

Looking at the high school ministry for First Church, it's readily apparent that it is top-heavy.

As is fairly typical with youth programs, the program at First Church is strongest at the shallowest levels of commitment. The ministry for First Church students at deeper levels of commitment is thin, centered mostly around two relatively short-term summer activities. (The Youth Choir can broaden the opportunities slightly, but only for students willing to participate in a choir-type activity.) Beyond these general observations, these are the kinds of specific questions one might consider:

■ Is the Sunday night youth fellowship really a Come Level event?

For that Sunday night fellowship to genuinely attract Come Level youth, it probably needs a pretty thorough overhaul, beginning with the name. Since when is an activity called "Youth Fellowship" a big draw to non-Christian, non-churched kids?

We do ourselves a disservice when we call Come Level events "United Methodist Youth Fellowship" or "Baptist Youth Fellowship." If we truly want to reach non-Methodist, or non-Baptist, or non-Christian students, that goal should be reflected in our name. A non-Christian teen would logically assume that a program called "Freaks for Jesus" is one in which they may not feel comfortable. That is why most youth workers I know do not attend conventions of the American Society of Civil Engineers. They assume that they don't belong there!

If an event is Come Level, it should be Come Level right down to the name. That's why Young Life is called Young Life. If you are young and alive, you're in! A name like "Sunday Night Live" or "Breakaway" would be much more appropriate if First Church really wants to make its Sunday night meeting a Come Level event.

Obviously, the nature of the event itself is even more important than the name. So often, youth workers have what they consider Come Level events, but the actual content and mood of the events is Grow or Disciple Level. For example, while visiting with one church youth group, I was interested to hear the youth leader repeatedly encourage his youth to invite their non-Christian friends to this weekly meeting. That led me to believe that this meeting would be Come Level in content.

I was surprised when the group began singing because their choice of songs was anything but Come Level. They sang "Father I Adore You," "He Is Lord," "Alleluia," and some other really beautiful songs of praise. But, songs of praise are more appropriate when Christians sing together. It doesn't seem fair to expect a non-Christian to come to a meeting to which he has been invited, and then force that student to sing praises to a God he is not even willing to recognize.

The real clincher came during about the third chorus when the youth leader looked up from his guitar, stopped the singing, stared straight at some of the guys in the back of the group and said, "You guys might be new here, but you need to get up off your rear and start singing or you can leave." Now here was a case where this youth leader unconsciously had betrayed these youth and those who had invited them.

Come Level kids, when they attend an activity, are not promising they will worship, sing, pray, or study the Bible. They are promising to be there as long as we have what they like. We need to welcome them on those terms. If they are not "fitting in" with what the group is doing, that may be the group's fault, not the students'. That's what it means to make a Come Level activity truly an activity for Come Level kids.

■ Does the basketball program really attract Come Level kids?

This is an easy question to answer, but also a very important one. If the basketball league is legitimately a Come Level program, it should be attracting new kids from First Church's Pool of Humanity. With the time, money, and energy it takes to actually run a good basketball program even in a small league, one needs to be sure one is getting what one has paid for.

If one discovers that the basketball program involves almost totally students already involved in other areas of the program, it might be wise to redesign the basketball program to fit the level of commitment of the kids involved. Realize that it isn't really a Come Level outreach, and remake it—perhaps into a Grow Level program. For example, it might be a requirement that any of the guys on the basketball team must also work through a workbook on Christian growth to maintain eligibility. Or requirements can include Scripture memory, a service project, or consistent attendance at the weekly Bible study.

■ Are Grow Level youth really the ones in Sunday School?

This may be the question that most needs to be asked of the average youth program. That's because Sunday School often is a classic case of providing a program that does not fit those in attendance. Common sense and experience tells us that, in most cases, Sunday School is probably the time during the week when our program draws the most genuinely Come Level students. Parents will force their kids to participate in Sunday School when they will not force them to be involved in any other area of the program. But, ironically, the average Sunday School consists largely of Grow Level (or deeper) study materials.

I'm convinced that one of the major reasons for so many of the discipline problems that confront Sunday School teachers is that they are trying to use Grow Level materials with Come Level students. That won't work! A person-oriented approach to Sunday School would be to admit that most of our participants are Come Level kids who are there begrudgingly, daring us to "bless" them. Then, change the format and content of Sunday School to more of a Come Level atmosphere. It may sound radical, but it certainly sounds reasonable.

This is the kind of thinking that we should be doing in stage three of the evaluation process to really find out if the program "runs." There are other questions that might be asked of the program at First Church, but let's shift our attention for the remaining chapters to some strategies that First Church could possibly use for programming at the Disciple Level and beyond.

■

WHAT ABOUT YOU?

Use this sheet for personal evaluation.

1. As you filled in the pyramids in this chapter, what did you discover about—

    ■ *The young people in your ministry?*

    ■ *The programs in your ministry?*

2. At what level is your highest concentration of young people?

    At what level do you have the highest concentration of programs?

3. Are any changes in program balance indicated when you study the pyramid on page 35? What changes might be appropriate?

4. How do your program levels and student levels match up? In other words, are your Come Level programs attracting Come Level kids? Are Disciple Level programs attended by Disciple Level kids?

5. In terms of time and money invested, at which level of programming is your ministry making the greatest investment? Does this investment reflect your vision and values?

CHAPTER SIX

Programming for Higher Levels of Commitment

The title of this chapter could be misleading because programs don't make disciples. Only disciples make disciples. But, the most capable disciple-maker in the world will be ineffective without some sort of plan or program for allowing this process to happen. This chapter is about three specific programs aimed at youth who are at commitment levels of Grow Level and higher.

Outlining specific programs can be dangerous. David tried to fight in Saul's armor (1 Sam. 17:38-39), and "could not, for he was not used to them." Sometimes, when we try to take someone else's program and use it in our ministry, it just doesn't work because we are trying to fight in someone else's armor. Some fight with armor, and some fight with a sling, but above all, everyone must use strategies that are comfortable for them.

At the same time, doing program evaluation and rethinking our ministry objectives won't be very helpful if we aren't able to implement some changes. On the following pages are descriptions and examples of three programs used by a particular church in a particular Pool of Humanity. While these models may need to be adapted so that the "armor" will fit your style and ministry, this will provide some practical models for actually developing programs that build disciples. The first two programs, Small Group and Covenant Group, are built around a fellowship group format. The third, Onward Bound, is a personally tailored program for spiritual growth.

Small Groups and Covenant Group: Two Programs That Worked

Dr. Merton Strommen, in his classic work, *Five Cries of Youth,* writes that the loudest of all the "five cries of youth" is the cry of self-hatred— young people trying to live with a self that they don't respect, don't admire, and can't exchange. Most interesting, though, is Strommen's insight about how we in youth ministry can respond to this attitude in our ministries with teens. "The techniques of hearty encouragement, bushels of compliments, and a series of social gatherings are not enough. Low self-esteem youth need a community or small group where they can live in the awareness of being accepted" (*Five Cries of Youth,* Strommen, Harper, p. 30).

For that reason, it's difficult to conceive of an effective youth program that does not make use of some kind of small group strategy. Obviously, if the youth group is small to begin with, it may not be necessary to design an actual program to fulfill this role. But, if there are more than ten youth involved, this might be a strategic way to move.

For the most part, any sort of serious small group program is going to be a Grow Level (or above) activity. That is the case simply because for any small group ministry to be effective, the participants must have some degree of willingness to maintain consistent attendance. Without the component of consistent attendance, the most creative small group in the world is doomed to failure.

Before we look at two specific small group-type strategies that can be used with Grow and Disciple Level students, let's think through some of the basic components of effective small groups. Purely and simply, small groups are about fellowship, what the New Testament characterizes as *koinonia*. While the church, in general, has horribly misused this term, nowhere has it been more misused than in youth ministry. We have Sunday night "fellowship." We "fellowship" around the bowling alley. And, sometimes we have "fellowship" during the twenty minutes between Sunday School and worship.

Howard Snyder has diagnosed the problem very clearly, "The church today is suffering a fellowship crisis. . . . It is simply not experiencing nor demonstrating that 'fellowship of the Holy Spirit' (2 Cor. 13:14) that marked the New Testament church. . . . The church is highly organized just at the time when her members are caring less about organization and more about community" (*The Problem with Wineskins,* Snyder, IVP, p. 89).

If this is true for the church in general, it is especially true for youth ministry. Donald Posterski, a leader in Canadian youth ministry, reports that his research for Project Teen Canada indicates there is no value that teenagers rank more highly than their small cluster of close friends. Posterski goes on to point out that his research shows that while kids certainly enjoy the big, rowdy group meetings where there is a large group of teenagers, over the long haul their preference is for small, informal groups. (As Posterski remarks, this represents a change from ten years ago when youth ministry capitalized more on a "herd mentality" that focused on a group of "in" kids who by their attendance might attract other kids who want to be associated with the popular crowd.)

Not only do small groups help us to minister to the area of "felt need" that Posterski points to, they help us to give unique focus to one of the three components of a discipleship lifestyle that we discussed earlier in this book. Most youth groups have some arena in which kids are being "taught" the Bible and, in most cases, there is every effort to apply that biblical teaching to daily life. But small groups give us the perfect setting to learn and develop body life.

What a Small Group IS NOT

Whenever we talked about small groups in our youth program, we always took pains to make sure that the students knew what we were about. We were careful to stress that this was not another Bible study. We tried, rather, to make our small groups "people studies" based on the Bible. We really felt that our students were getting enough Bible study. Small Group was where we focused on "Body study." That is an important balance to be maintained.

We wanted to emphasize that small groups in our program were not there strictly for socializing. This was not some kind of Christian fraternity within the youth group. While the intention was to leave the groups unstructured enough to promote open spontaneous sharing, we reminded leaders of the old law: "One of the best ways to guarantee spontaneity is to plan very carefully." Our small group ministries were designed specifically to open students to one another.

Finally, we needed to make it clear that small group ministry is not some kind of mystical "navel gazing" where people sit around in a circle and do cute things like shaping their bubble gum into their image of love. Too much of what the church has tried to do under the guise of "fellowship" has not been biblical sharing in which brothers and sisters come together around the lordship of Christ. Ultimately, the purpose of our small group ministries was to bring students closer to the members of the body of Christ so that they could grow closer to the Christ of the body.

What a Small Group IS

As general guidelines for structuring an effective small group ministry, consider these five components (taken from *Sixty-Nine Ways to Start a Small Group and Keep It Growing,* Larry Richards, Zondervan):

Identification. A sound small group program will build in ways for teens to identify themselves. This is as much for their own benefit as it is for the others in the small group. Every person needs to understand the difference between history (facts about birthday, parent's occupation, grade in school, etc.) and "his story" ("who I am," "where I'm going," and "why I'm me").

Affirmation. We need to help kids come up with ways of making affirming statements about their brothers and sisters in Christ without feeling strange. Typically, the guys are afraid to compliment a girl because they are afraid the girls will think they're in love. And, of course, the girls have that same fear of being overly admiring. We have to give them ways and means of affirming who they are once they've identified themselves. This concept that "these people know the real me, and like me" is a tremendous point of awakening for most teenagers.

Exploration. This component of small groups deals with the continuing need to give students avenues by which they can explore themselves, their feelings, and their values, while learning about the others in the group.

Concentration. This is that dimension of a small group that keeps it focused. The concentration of the small group should be Scripture, and how that Scripture can be used to help them probe and understand their lives as Christians.

Adoration. As the group grows together, there should be an increasing amount of time spent in prayer and praise. This accomplishes two things:

(1) It helps students begin to feel comfortable talking about spiritual matters and praying together, a dimension that becomes increasingly important as they grow into more leadership/Develop Level-type roles; and
(2) this helps them to move into the Disciple Level of commitment because it teaches them how to practice the discipline of worship and prayer.

WANTED: Lifelines of Love

Dear UMYF Friends:

Over the last year we have heard more and more people share that they would like to see us add one thing to our UMYF program that we really don't have. People have shared that even though they are enjoying the weekly Bible studies at Cornerstone and that it's really neat to have all those people up in the Teen Room on Sunday nights when we have BREAKAWAY there still isn't any opportunity during the week for people to *get together and just share.* If you try to do that on Wednesday night after Bible Study, you flunk a test the next day, and if you try to do that on Sunday night before Breakaway you're liable to get a Ping-Pong ball hit down your throat.

So.......

..........Last year we started trying to build some *Lifelines of love,* some groups for good, honest sharing. And that was the beginning of our SMALL GROUP program.

A SMALL GROUP IS: a group of friends who meet together on a weekly basis, share their lives (the good and the bad), and pray for each other. It is led by one of our older UMYF members and the group agrees to meet for at least 13 weeks together.

A SMALL GROUP IS NOT: another Bible study, a gossip committee, or just a group of guys to hang around with. You are making a commitment to those in your group to try and be there every week for 13 weeks, and take part in the group.

If you think you may be interested in a SMALL GROUP, fill in the blanks and *turn it in to Duffy before Jan. 9.* You will be assigned to a group on the basis of your sex, which day you can meet, and other secret factors.

I'm interested in being in a **SMALL GROUP**:

Name _____

Male   Female (circle one)   Grade _____

Phone _____

Best day for me to meet:
Mon. Tues. Wed. Thur. Fri. Sat.
(Circle one)

I'd like _____ to be in my group with me.

In an attempt to develop a small group program for our ministry that would incorporate all of the five components of effective small groups, one youth program I worked with created a program that we called (in a stroke of magnificent creativity) Small Groups! In the interest of building a program that would best meet the needs of our group, the Small Group program had three basic agendas.

- We needed a small group program for our younger teens, a program that did not involve coed groups. For the junior high kids, especially the guys, we felt this would provide an environment more conducive to honest sharing.

- We needed a small group program that would not require Disciple Level commitment, a program in which there were few requirements other than consistent attendance. Most of our young junior highers were not Disciple Level yet.

- We needed to provide an arena in which our Develop and Multiplier Level youth could begin to exercise and sharpen ministry skills. By leading these small groups, they were able to test their abilities to deal with Scripture, nurture younger Christians, and take spiritual responsibility for their own peers.

The program designed to meet the needs was a small group program open to junior and senior high school students, small groups that would be segregated according to sex. We decided to use this formula for group makeup because we knew that to really develop a group in which junior high students would feel open to share, the groups should be set up on a same-sex basis.

In promoting Small Groups, there was an initial mailing to all of our youth giving a fairly clear description of the program (see "Wanted: Lifelines . . ." which is a slightly revised version of our actual handout). The one and only requirement for participants was consistent attendance. In the information we were careful to stipulate that Small Groups would involve a 13-week commitment. It's important to make clear that the students are not being asked to commit the rest of their natural lives to the Small Group. Without that assurance, some kids who might otherwise get involved would assess the cost and risk of commitment as being too high.

In signing up for Small Group, students could note their choices in three particular areas: (1) group leader; (2) one best friend who would definitely be in their group; and (3) what day of the week they would like to meet. While we did not want to put best-friend cliques together, we knew that this choice, assuring them of at least one good friend in their group, would defuse some of their fears about signing up.

Leadership for these groups was provided by some of the Develop and Multiplier Level students in our program. These students were recruited by the youth leader in a low-key, non-democratic way! Small Group leaders met once a month for training, sharing, and trouble-shooting.

Leaders were instructed that their role was not to give a weekly Bible study. (We didn't feel we could expect them to offer a Bible study every week unless we provided more adult leadership and supervision.) Rather, their role was to lead weekly "people-studies" based around the Bible. In other words, their task was to encourage students to share about their own lives, but center their sharing around one or two particular Bible verses.

"The Permanent Press"

For example, a Small Group leader might use the following text as the focus verse: "Not that I have already obtained it, or have already become perfect, but I press on in order that I may lay hold of that for which also I was laid hold of by Christ Jesus. Brethren, I do not regard myself as having laid hold of it yet; but one thing I do: forgetting what lies behind and reaching forward to what lies ahead, I press on toward the goal for the prize of the upward call of God in Christ Jesus" (Phil. 3:12-14).

Based on that verse, the Small Group leader might give these instructions to the group: "Paul's emphasis here is about being consistent in your walk with Christ. It's almost like you could entitle this passage "The Permanent Press." But let's think about our own spiritual lives. I just wonder, if washing instructions came with your spiritual life, what kind of instructions would be given? Here are some options:

- *Permanent press*—ready to wear,
- *Dry clean only*—excessive stretching may rip seams,
- *Delicate*—suited for lukewarm handling,
- *Wash carefully*—apt to fade,
- *Hang dry only*—may shrink in intense heat.

"I'd like you guys to use this as a springboard and share with the group why one of those sets of instructions might come with your spiritual life."

Without going into the dynamics of small groups, this gives some idea of the kind of material that was used in Small Group. Sometimes, students prepared their own materials, but they were free to get materials from the youth office or from volunteers. Essentially, it was the job of the adult leadership to facilitate the leadership ministry of our students.

One of the ways this adult "oversight" was built in was by assigning one adult volunteer to each Small Group leader as a Small Group Overseer. Using the contact sheet (example on the following page) these Overseers were responsible for phoning their Small Group leader once a week to encourage them, to see if they had special concerns or needs, and to build in some accountability.

CONTACT SHEET

Small Group Overseer _____ Group Members _____
                          (your name)
Small Group Leader(s) _____ _____ _____
                      _____ _____ _____

Leader's Name	Date Contacted	Report	Needs	Comment

THE Covenant GROUP

Covenant *(Kuv'e-nant)*, n. a written agreement; a deed; a free promise of God's blessing; a solemn agreement of fellowship and faith between members of a church.

YOU ARE INVITED to be part of an experiment in spiritual adventure . . . not something for everybody . . . a challenge . . . an exercise in commitment and faith . . . a solemn agreement of fellowship and faith between members of Christ's body!

The **COVENANT GROUP** is simply a group of people who are willing to make a 13-week agreement or covenant with each other that they will genuinely seek to (a) grow in their relationships with Christ individually, and (b) grow in their relationships with each other as a group. In the last year there have been a number in our UMYF who point to the Covenant Group as the most meaningful experience they have had in their walks with Christ.

The Covenant Group *IS NOT* some kind of "spiritual Green Berets" or "Superheroes"—it is a group of people serious about making a 13-week commitment to maintain certain disciplines. Basically, those in the Covenant Group are 9th-12th-graders who are willing to make a "solemn agreement" to:

(1) Consistently attend *CORNERSTONE* and *BREAKAWAY* each week. In addition, Covenanters must attend a special retreat (no cost to you) on May 11-12, 1984.

(2) Attend a weekly Tuesday morning breakfast at church before school beginning at 6:30. The first breakfast will be on Tuesday morning, January 24. You will be expected to be at the breakfast consistently and *ON TIME* (please note this).

(3) Practice the discipline of a daily Quiet Time *and* bring with you each Tuesday morning an entry into a Quiet Time Diary or personal spiritual journal to be kept during the nine weeks.

(4) Enroll in the "Onward Bound" Program. Information available from Youth Office.

If you wish to make such a commitment or covenant, sign here and return this entire sheet to Duffy. It will be returned to you at our first prayer and sharing breakfast on Tuesday morning, January 24, 6:30.

NAME

Covenant Group

We developed a second type of small group ministry that was designed particularly for students at the Disciple Level, a ministry we called Covenant Group. Covenant Group was a coed small group that involved quite a bit more commitment than Small Group, and was open only to high school students.

The basic requirements of the program were simple, but important. Students who were unfaithful to the terms of the covenant were encouraged to either become more faithful or withdraw until such time as they could genuinely fulfill the terms of the agreement. To make sure that Covenant Group did not become some sort of "spiritual green berets," we required all CG members to consistently attend our weekly Bible study, Cornerstone, and our weekly Come Level meeting, Breakaway. (See sample Covenant agreement on page 48.)

Covenant Group members were also required to keep a journal or diary of their devotional thoughts and insights. This was done to (a) insure that they were building a pattern of daily devotions, and (b) because it was important for them to give some reflection about what God was doing in their lives so that they would have something significant to share when they came to a weekly Tuesday morning meeting of the group.

This helped us to keep sharing to the point, and it limited the number of prayer requests related to diseases and sicknesses of relatives. (It is, of course, much easier for kids to make those kinds of requests than to share their own struggles and needs.)

The Covenant Group met once a week for breakfast and sharing together. Eating the breakfast may have been the toughest requirement of all! The cold cereal and overdone buns made a breakfast that only the spiritually hearty would tolerate. But the sharing and prayer were warm and precious. Students would work their way around the table, reading their journals, some sharing an insight from Scripture, another asking for prayer, and another talking about something he had learned from a Christian book he was reading through for Onward Bound (next chapter). Many times there were tears. Many times laughter. Always there was love, acceptance, honest sharing, and a genuine experience of the "fellowship of the Holy Spirit."

At the completion of the 13-week Covenant agreement, students could either "reenlist" or they could withdraw without any sense of guilt or pressure. Always, at the end of our thirteen weeks, we celebrated our group and our experience with a one-night retreat that was low-budget, low-key, and very low-programming.

This retreat allowed the group time for reflection on our common and individual experiences. I've seen huge crowds at Come Level events, hilarious skits, and super ski weekends, but I can say without question that these one-night retreats were some of the most meaningful hours of youth ministry I've known.

The final element of Covenant Group in which students were required to take part was Onward Bound. This program is explained in the next chapter.

CHAPTER SEVEN

Onward Bound: A Program of Personal Growth and Discipleship

Sally is a junior in high school. Two years ago at our winter retreat, Sally made a very genuine and life-changing decision to be a follower of Jesus Christ. In a lot of ways, she's a youth worker's dream. She's active in our program. She reaches out to her friends at school. Her daily time in the Word is at a level of consistency that I had reached by my second year of seminary!

Sally's problem is that she is very weak in the area of personal management. She arrives late to meetings, if she remembers to come at all, and she is generally undependable. Her grades have been slipping at school, and at home her room has been investigated by the EPA as a possible site for Superfund clean-up. Not only has all of this disorganization begun to affect her relationships with parents and friends, it's beginning to bother Sally and affect the way she thinks about herself.

"But if she's not on drugs and having sex . . ."

Five years ago, I would have dealt with Sally in one of two equally unproductive ways:

(1) *"Sally is a typical teenager."* I would have shrugged my shoulders and shaken my head, having resigned myself to the fact that "kids are kids" and that as long as Sally wasn't on drugs or sexually involved with some guy, then I was doing my job. My prayer for Sally would have been that "she will grow up and act like an adult." (It never occurred to me then that it is that attitude that has produced so many adults who act like teenagers!) I really never thought of Sally's "decision to be a follower of Christ" as being something that would reach into the mundane affairs of personal management.

(2) *"Sally needs to be reconverted."* I might have assumed that Sally "just isn't serious about the Lord. If, after all, she were really sold out to Jesus, she would be dealing with these problem areas." Somehow, maybe we were wrong about Sally's decision on that winter retreat. I might have dealt with Sally by assuming that she had fallen away from her commitment to Christ, or that perhaps her conversion just wasn't real enough or deep enough.

Two Common Mistakes

Each of these approaches to Sally's growing pains represents two very common errors related to the spiritual growth of teenagers.

Problem number one:
We ignore the fact that spiritual growth is practical. Samuel Chadwick, a godly preacher of the eighteenth century, reportedly used to pray, "Lord, make us intensely spiritual, thoroughly practical, and perfectly natural." He understood that holiness is not an obsolete monastic discipline that wouldn't play out in daily life. Biblical holiness should affect every dimension of life, and so should it be in the lives of our youth. We have mistakenly believed or implied that having sex too soon is a spiritual problem, but that getting to an appointment too late is not.

The Apostle Paul said, "I decided to know nothing among you except Christ and Him crucified" (1 Corinthians 2:2, RSV), but he went on to speak in that same letter about widely ranging issues of practical lifestyle. I was encouraging Sally to be intensely spiritual. I'm not sure I knew how to help her make holiness thoroughly practical.

Problem number two:
We forget that spiritual growth is a process. With all of our talk about the difference that Christ can make in a student's life, we've forgotten that spiritual growth takes time. I like to remind kids of God's words in Deuteronomy 7:22-23 that "the Lord your God will clear away these nations before you little by little; you will not be able to put an end to them quickly, lest the wild beasts grow too numerous for you" (NASB). Spiritual growth is a process of attacking one beast at a time.

Like so many Christian teenagers in our youth groups, Sally did not need to be "reconverted" (whatever that means). Sally was tuned to the right channel, but to make the image still clearer, she needed some fine-tuning. Unfortunately, youth ministry in most churches seems to be geared to channel-changing. We have not been very effective with fine-tuning.

The Fine Art of Fine-Tuning

Fine-tuning is a one-to-one process. In trying to meet Sally's needs, most of us might initiate a series of Bible studies about time management or "doing all things heartily, as serving God and not men" (based on Colossians 3:23), and that's great. But what about John who is just as interested in spiritual growth as Sally, but the beast he needs to attack is a bad relationship with his sister? And then there's Steve who is a fantastic kid, really loves the Lord, but can't seem to work out his relationship with his parents. The problem with fine-tuning is that it varies for each receiver. It is not a group activity. We need to find a way to meet the unique fine-tuning needs of each of the youth in our program.

Fine-tuning takes time. The reason that we don't give more attention to this sort of ministry is that it is very time-consuming. Fine-tuning takes careful listening. Trying to do this kind of ministry without the aid of a volunteer team is impossible except for the smallest of programs.

To help the Sallys and Steves and Johns deal with their problems requires accountability. It is not enough to suggest strategies of dealing with these issues. There need to be occasions for frequent "checking-in."

Fine-tuning takes creativity. It's not so hard to keep Sally away from drugs; there's material available. There are books and studies to use. A lot of the work has been done. As I began to work with some of these areas of fine-tuning, I realized that this would be more difficult. Publishers don't sense as broad a market for the fine-tuning issues, so there is less material. Moreover, I learned quickly that if we were going to effect a change in behavior, we were going to have to do more than assign books to read or verses to memorize. That demands creativity.

Onward Bound

With all of these factors in mind, we developed a program of personal growth and discipleship. Based on Paul's statements in Philippians 3:12-14, we used this program to stress the ongoing process of spiritual growth and commitment for the long haul. This program, Onward Bound, was open to any students interested in a growth plan that would be personally tailored to meet their needs. The students were told up front that it would be time-consuming, and that they were expected to make and keep a thirteen-week commitment to the program.

Phase one: Evaluation

We used a three-phase strategy with each youth who signed on. Phase One involved *evaluation*. The first step was to help each student explore and consider areas in which they needed to grow. This was done using four sources of input:

- *Taylor-Johnson temperament analysis.* Each student was given this rather simple test to help them get a self-portrait of their temperament. This particular instrument evaluates traits like Nervous versus Composed, Active-Social versus Quiet, Depressive versus Light-hearted, Hostile versus Tolerant, Self-Disciplined versus

A PROGRAM OF PERSONAL GROWTH AND DISCIPLESHIP

If you are a person committed to Jesus Christ . . . committed to growth . . . committed to being stretched by God's Word and God's Spirit . . . open to "pressing on" in your walk with Christ, *then,* ONWARD BOUND *is for you!*

"I do not claim that I have already become perfect. I press on for the prize of the upward call of God in Christ Jesus. Of course, my brothers, I really do not think that I have made it; the one thing I do, however, is to forget what is behind me and do my best to reach what is ahead."

—Paul (Phil. 3:12-14)

What is Onward Bound?—Onward Bound is a totally new program for the UMYF, but the concept is as old as Christianity. Onward Bound is a program designed to meet the needs of the many in our fellowship who are eager and ready to chart a course of personal Christian growth for themselves, that will help them to focus specifically on some areas in which they personally need to grow.

Who can take part in the Onward Bound program?—The Onward Bound program is open to every member of our UMYF Fellowship but that doesn't mean everybody should do it. There are some in our group who, in addition to the regular Bible studies, etc. we have each week at Cornerstone and Sunday School, desire to get some individual encouragement and guidance for areas that they really want to zero in on. It will require commitment, and some time to meet with your growth partner at least once every week or two.

How does it work?—Onward Bound consists of two phases: (1) Evaluation: Finding some areas in which you feel you need to grow; helping each person discover some areas that need work which the person might not even be aware of; spending some time considering your strengths and weaknesses. (2) Focus: Choosing an area to really focus in on; discussing this area with Duffy and your growth partner and determining a growth strategy that will involve Scripture memorization, sharing what you've learned with others, reading some material that may help you work on the area you've chosen, and then putting what you've learned into practice.

How do I join?—Just sign your name on the form below, and then make an interview appointment with Duffy *immediately*.

ONWARD BOUND: _____ **Phone:** _____

Impulsive, etc. While this is a helpful tool, the particular instrument used is not that important. Students who enrolled in the program the second year were given a "Spiritual Life Check-up" prepared by Dennis Wayman (see *Leadership,* Fall, 1983) which was equally helpful.

- *Parental evaluation forms.* The parents of each student were sent a short letter, signed by the student, asking for their honest input about various elements of the student's personal habits (use of free time, accepting responsibility around the house, keeping room acceptable, contributing to unity and health of the family, etc.). The letter made it clear that these responses would be shared with the students.

- *Personal interview.* This interview provided two final sources of input: (1) The students were given the results of both their Taylor-Johnson analyses and the parental evaluation forms and asked where they felt they needed work; (2) Secondly, as the youth minister, I gave them my evaluation of where they needed to grow.

Phase two: Growth Contract

Based on the above information, we moved to phase two: *Drawing up a growth contract.* For each student, a personally tailored program of growth was created. (See the sample blank contract on p. 55.) This Growth Contract involved at least four categories of focus:

- *Scripture.* Each contract involved some element of Bible study or memorization, or both.

- *Reading.* Students were assigned a book or articles that would give some insight into the area with which they struggled.

- *Life.* Each student was given some assignment that had to do with actually putting their growth goals into some observable behavior. This might involve keeping a log of how many arguments Steve has with his parents in the next two weeks, listing the time, the circumstances, subject, and result of the disagreement. That gave the student a chance to observe his or her behavior more objectively, and it often showed us ways that reconciliation could take place.

- *Sharing.* Each student was assigned some area in which to share his or her goals and how each was working to grow through personal struggles. A student might share with his small group one thing learned from each of the chapters in the book he was assigned to read.

Phase three: Accountability

During phase three, over the course of the next thirteen weeks, each student met with one of the ministry team members semiweekly. These Growth Partners were responsible for seeing that each student was making progress in his or her contract, and even more so, helping students to reflect on what they were learning through their various assignments. These meetings usually lasted an hour-and-a-half, and they were the absolute key to the effectiveness of the strategy.

Signs of Progress

For the first time, we were seeing some real progress in some of the trouble areas that had been so elusive for our kids. They sensed the growth in their own lives and were able to see the practical implications of spirituality on a daily basis. Needless to say, it was helpful to our leaders in that it gave them a format for working with students one-on-one.

An unexpected by-product of the program was the renewed parental support. Parents sensed this was one tangible way we were working with them to nurture their child. Another unexpected dividend was the increase in reading Christian books. As kids shared how Tim Stafford's book, *The Trouble with Parents,* had been helpful to them, other students wanted to read it. We developed a library out of the youth office.

ONWARD BOUND - Parents' Input Form

Dear Mom/Dad:

Please fill out the evaluation form below as honestly and completely as you can. Your input will help me evaluate points on which I want to focus in my Onward Bound Growth Contract. Duffy will share your input with me, so please be as specific and as honest as you can be. I understand that your comments are made in love, and I know that you understand that I ask for this input so that I can continue to tune up my relationship with my family and my Lord.

Sincerely,

. . . .

■ FAMILY RELATIONSHIPS

1. I feel that my son/daughter is considerate of the rights and feelings of other family members.
2. _____ is willing to share himself with other family members.
3. _____ is willing to assume his share of responsibility in our family by helping around the house.
4. _____ contributes to the spiritual atmosphere in our household.

■ PERSONAL HABITS

1. _____ is disciplined in the management of his time.
2. _____ wastes a lot of time by watching TV or talking on the phone more than I feel he/she should.
3. _____ seems to be doing his/her best in whatever task he/she undertakes.
4. _____ does his/her best to keep his/her room clean and presentable(!).

Very True	Usually True	Sometimes	Not Often

GENERAL COMMENTS

Are there other areas where you would like to see some work? What do you observe as your son/daughter's greatest strengths? Any other comments or explanation of above answers?

PARENTS: This form is not confidential. I will share the results with your son/daughter. But, please return it to Duffy Robbins c/o Wilmore UMC, P.O. Box 68 by mail. Thanks for your help.

Warning

As with any system, the results are only as good as the people running the system. The Growth Partners can make or break the whole idea. Secondly, it is vital that students be forced to shape very specific growth goals going into phase three. It's too easy to say, "I want to be more of a blessing to my family." Accountability is almost impossible with a goal like that. Ed and Bobbie Reeds' criteria (*Creative Bible Learning for Youth,* Gospel Light/ICL) for choosing good objectives are helpful here. Students should be encouraged to use goals that are measurable (one can know if one has reached them), reachable (it is possible to accomplish this in thirteen weeks), and ownable (it is the student's goal and not what the student thinks I want him to choose for a goal).

A final caution is that spiritual growth doesn't come through programs; it comes through people. Onward Bound is simply a structure designed to meet a need. A different need might call for a completely different structure or for an adaptation of the one given here. The key is to find some means of encouraging our students to grow progressively into the image of Christ.

Sally doesn't need to be ignored until she has a drastic breakdown. Nor does she need to be nagged into reconversion so that *this* time she can really, really, really get serious about Jesus. Like most growing things, Sally needs nurture, care, pruning, and the right environment.

Growth Contract

"I do not claim that I have already become perfect. I press on for the prize of the upward call of God in Christ Jesus. Of course, my brothers, I really do not think that I have made it; the one thing I do, however, is to forget what is behind me and do my best to reach what lies ahead."—Paul (Phil. 3:12-14)

Date _____

Please complete this growth contract carefully, prayerfully, and completely. This is a covenant, a contract, A PROMISE, that to the best of your ability, with God's help, you will complete the contract below. This contract is based on areas of growth that you have pinpointed for special concentration. Be willing to push yourself. Your Growth Partner is taking valuable time to meet with you. Make those meetings count. Try to meet with him/her a minimum of three times, four times if possible.

I, _____, in an effort to "press on for the prize of the upward call of God in Christ Jesus," do solemnly commit myself, with God's help, to grow in the following areas of my life. I understand that I will be held accountable for these goals and that my contract to grow in these areas is not to be taken lightly.

REMEMBER: BE SPECIFIC!!

Goal One: _____

_____

Goal Two: _____

_____

Goal Three: _____

_____

It is *my responsibility* to meet with my growth partner. I will be responsible for setting up meetings on the following days/times:

No. 1 _____ No. 2 _____ No. 3 _____ No. 4 _____

This contract is to be finished by _____ (Date).
In order to make progress toward these goals I have stated, I will work in the following growth areas with the assignments listed below:

SCRIPTURE: _____

_____

PRACTICE: _____

_____

READING: _____

_____

SHARING: _____

_____

© 1987 by SP Publications, Inc. Permission granted to purchaser to reproduce this sheet for use in ministry to youth.

CHAPTER EIGHT

Personal Reflection

■ The quick answers never seem to work very well in youth ministry. Experience teaches most of us that lesson sooner or later. But, even more so, my experience has taught me that the most fitting answer, or the most practical program, will accomplish very little if it isn't infused with the Spirit of God. Anyone who attempts to use these ideas without spending some serious time on his or her knees is probably going to find them as dry and lifeless as last year's bird's nest!

Even with fervent and consistent prayer, though, there are times when youth ministry can be woefully frustrating. For that reason, I'd like to close this book with an excerpt from the *Addresses and Papers of John R. Mott* (yes, it is a catchy title!). Mott, of course, was one of the pioneers of the Student Christian Movement that led hundreds of men and women to the mission field around the turn of this century. Though his own mission work was largely in China, his impact was, quite literally, worldwide. Near the end of his life, Mott wrote the following lines in his journal:

> *As I lay thinking this afternoon I asked myself, "What would I do if I had my life to live over again?" I would give vastly more emphasis and concentration upon schoolboys. This vision-forming period when the character and aims of life is shaped is of primary and central importance. For instance, if asked what I would do in China, I would pick 100 of the strongest men and women of the West and ask them to give themselves entirely to the service of the high school boys and girls in the government schools of that country.*

The first time I read that quote, I was struck almost simultaneously with two thoughts that have consistently challenged me. To begin with I was impressed with how different might the world be today if John R. Mott had followed through on that vision earlier in his life. How might history have been radically changed? How different our current world situation might be if Mott had given himself "entirely" to the student population of China in the early 1900s. After all, that is the generation that has leadership in that massive nation even today. But, of course, I was immediately confronted with the realization that now the opportunity has passed. It's too late for John R. Mott. That's when I was confronted with this second thought: *It's not too late for us!* We can still make a difference. By the power of God, we can even change history.

For my money, that's why youth ministry is so exciting. That's why I'm so encouraged that there are people willing to "give themselves entirely to the service of the high school boys and girls" of this country.

With the conclusion of this book, I want to encourage my brothers and sisters in youth ministry to take full advantage of our opportunity now. How tragic that, in years to come, we might look back like Mott with all his accomplishments, and lament that because we had been under-committed to youth ministry, we had overlooked great opportunity for the Gospel. I hope and pray that we'll continue to be haunted and challenged by that vision.

■

BIBLIOGRAPHY
Materials for Student Growth

This is by no means a complete or exhaustive bibliography. There is new attention being given by publishers to the needs of not only the youth worker, but the youth with whom he or she works. Since this group of people—namely, teenagers who read Christian books—is still not a very large market, there is very little promotion and writing aimed at this market. It is out of that reality that this bibliography is being developed.

Books are arranged under general topical headings.

PERSONAL DISCIPLESHIP/BIBLE STUDY BOOKS

Discussion Manual for Student Relationships
Dawson McAllister, Shepherd Productions, Inc., Estes Park, Colo. 1978.

Discussion Manual for Student Discipleship (Volumes 1 and 2)
Dawson McAllister, Shepherd Productions, Inc., Estes Park, Colo. 1978.

This is a series of three study manuals, fairly well-known by most folks in youth ministry. Their strength is that they cover a wide variety of topics germane to a teenager's lifestyle issues. A particular chapter can be assigned to a particular youth for his particular area of focus.

So You Want Solutions
So You Want to Get into the Race
So You Want to Set the Pace
Chuck Klein, Tyndale House Publishers, Wheaton, Ill. 1982.

These three study booklets take a young Christian from the basics of the faith to the basics of how to disciple others. The final chapter of the third book is "Dare to Multiply." Klein seems to put more emphasis on the latter stages of "how to disciple your friends" while McAllister deals more with topical issues (though McAllister has some good stuff on this too: i.e., one chapter from vol. 2 entitled, "How to Start Your Own Ministry."

Discovering God's Will
Experiencing God's Attributes
Experiencing God's Presence
Warren and Ruth Myers, NavPress, Colorado Springs, Colo. 1983.

Warren and Ruth Myers' "Experiencing God Series" is an excellent set of three study books for the youth motivated enough to do some extra digging and thinking. Not recommended for everybody. This series will be treasured by mature high school-age Christians who are disciplined enough to think and meditate, and be nourished without spoon-feeding.

Moving Toward Maturity Series
Barry St. Clair, Victor Books, Wheaton, Ill.

This is a five-volume series, very practical for a growing Christian teenager. Covers a variety of topics as well as the basics of growth. Also offers some good instruction on the how-to of Bible study.

Design for Discipleship
Studies in Christian Living
NavPress, Colorado Springs, Colo.

These are two separate series of seven books and nine books, respectively. These studies are not particularly written for a teenage audience, but there is no reason why they can't be used effectively by teens. There is not the attention given to graphics and cartoons that one finds in other study-type booklets designed for teens. But the material is good. Some people shy away from using these books because they come in a series. The other side of that is that one can buy one of the books in the series to address a specific need rather than having to buy a more expensive booklet from a three-volume set. The latter books in each series require a strong commitment on the part of the user to dig for him or herself. The latter books in the *Studies . . .* series will lead a person into fairly deep inductive Bible study.

Discipleship! A Life Imperative
Barry St. Clair, Reach Out Ministries, Avondale Estates, Ga. 1980.

This five-booklet series is very much like the NavPress series though it is designed more for the junior and senior higher.

Breakthrough
Kent Fishel, Discipleship, Inc., Fort Wayne, Ind. 1982.

This is a three-part set that is set in a slightly different format that might make it more accessible to junior high students. The studies are not as demanding, but the material is solid and very practical. Could be used by a student on a daily basis for his quiet time.

Faith That Works
Andrew T. and Phyllis J. LePeau
Learning to Love God
Learning to Love People
Learning to Love Myself
Richard Peace
Fruits of the Spirit
Hazel Offner
In Spirit and in Truth
Wiliam Edgar, InterVarsity Press, Downers Grove, Ill.

These are but a few of the many personal and/or small group study booklets available from IVP. These are written primarily for college-age and older, but many of them are understandable and profitable for high school-age Christians. A catalog of materials is available from InterVarsity Press (see address at end of bibliography).

Young Disciples
Joyce Marie Smith, Tyndale House, Wheaton, Ill. 1983.

This is one of the booklets in Tyndale's "Good Life Bible Studies" series. While these can be used for group Bible studies, they are very usable for personal Bible study as well. These studies are specifically designed for students 12-16 years old, though more mature high schoolers may find them a bit too elementary.

The Love One Another Bible Study
Churches Alive, San Bernardino, Calif. 1979.

A set of seven group or individual studies (excellent for small groups), with booklets entitled **Forgiving, Communicating, Esteeming, Understanding, Submitting, Contributing,** and **Maintaining Unity.** An excellent resource.

HOW TO STUDY THE BIBLE

The Navigator Bible Studies Handbook
NavPress, Colorado Springs, Colo. 1975.
First-Hand Joy
Rick Yohn, NavPress, Colorado Springs, Colo. 1982.

Both of these books are excellent resources for equipping students and leaders to study the Bible for themselves. Rick Yohn's book is perhaps more appropriate for the high schooler.

Effective Bible Study
Howard Vos
How to Study the Bible
John B. Job
How to Understand Your Bible
Norton Sterrett, InterVarsity Press, Downers Grove, Ill.

These three books may be too advanced for most teens. There are some, however, who will benefit from these excellent books which are actually written for college-age and older.

John: A Daily Dialogue with God
Whitney Kuniholm, Harold Shaw Publishers, Wheaton, Ill. 1982.

This book takes a new direction in leading its readers through inductive, in-depth Bible study while set in the format of a devotional time. The studies are set up for a daily 20-40 minute "dialogue with God" using the Gospel of John. High schoolers will find this book very helpful.

DEVOTIONAL LIFE AND QUIET TIME

Prayer: More Than Words
Leroy Eims, NavPress, Colorado Springs, Colo. 1982.

Spending Time Alone with God
Barry St. Clair, Victor Books, Wheaton, Ill. 1983.

This is a practical book written for teens to guide them in the "what," "why," and "how" of a devotional life. (Volume two of the Moving Toward Maturity series.) A good book to give a teenager.

Devotions for Early Teens
Ruth Johnson, Moody Press, Chicago. 1972.

Practice to Win
Larry Jones, Tyndale House, Wheaton, Ill. 1983.

Good devotional book for your student athletes.

Pursuit of Holiness
Practice of Godliness
Jerry Bridges, Navpress, Colorado Springs, Colo. 1978.

Neither of these books has really been written for teens but older teens will find them helpful. Since these books come with study guides, it is possible to recommend the book to a student for his or her own use, and then suggest that they use the study guide to lead a small group using the book.

SELF-IMAGE

How to Make People Like You When You Know They Don't
Bob and Marilyn Donahue, Tyndale House Publishers, Wheaton, Ill. 1982.

A very good book for young adolescents who can't figure out why "nobody likes me." Practical and humorous.

Love Yourself
Walter Trobisch, InterVarsity Press, Downers Grove, Ill. 1976.

May be too advanced for most teens, but as with anything by Trobisch, the material is great.

How Can I Be Real?
Larry Richards, Zondervan, Grand Rapids, Mich. 1978.

Why Am I Afraid to Tell You Who I Am?
John Powell, S.J., Argus Communications, Allen, Texas. 1969.

A simple book with lots of colorful graphics and very easy reading.

TIME MANAGEMENT

The Christian Student's How to Study Guide
Jerry White, NavPress, Colorado Springs, Colo. 1980.

Once again, this is a book written primarily for college students, but many of its insights and hints are applicable to the high school teen.

Survive: The Art of Getting through High School
John Souter, Tyndale House, Wheaton, Ill. 1983.

Not really confined to Time Management, but has some good clues about how to take tests, improve memory, etc. Written for the high schooler.

Getting Your Act Together
Bob and Marilyn Donahue, Tyndale, Wheaton, Ill. 1982.

Another in the series of books written by the Donahues. This book is funny, but it offers some serious clues for a junior higher who wants to "get his or her act together."

MISCELLANEOUS

How Can I Make Decisions?
Larry Richards, Zondervan, Grand Rapids, Mich. 1980.

Secrets of the Christian Life
Philip Yancey, Zondervan/Campus Life, Grand Rapids, Mich. 1979.

What's the Good Word? The All New Super Incredible Bible Study Book for Junior Highs
John Souter, Zondervan, Grand Rapids, Mich. 1983.

This is a remarkably creative, innovative Bible survey for junior highers.

Beauty Care for the Tongue
LeRoy Koopman, Zondervan, Grand Rapids, Mich. 1979.

Devotional study of the tongue and speech habits. Can be used for group studies. Also in this series, **Beauty Care for the Ears, Beauty Care for the Eyes,** and **Beauty Care for the Hands.** Good books.

The Bible in Counseling
Waylon Ward, Moody Press, Chicago, Ill. 1977.

A youth worker can use this book as a resource in giving "homework" to a student depending on which areas he or she chooses to focus. This book offers Bible studies on self-image, guilt, fear, etc. It is not written for teens, but a youth worker can use the book with teens.

Your Family
Jim Conway and others, InterVarsity Press, Downers Grove, Ill. 1982.

Written for college and older, but individual articles may be helpful for teens to read.

GROUP STUDIES

In addition to the materials already mentioned. . . .

Campus Life LUG Manual (Volumes 1 and 2)
Edited by Bill Muir and Art Deyo, Youth for Christ, Wheaton, Ill. 1980.

A number of studies that a student can use in leading a small group. Very good resource.

Serendipity Studies
Lyman Coleman, Serendipity House, Littleton, Colo. 1982.

There are nine studies in the Serendipity Youth Bible Study Series. Some feared that earlier Serendipity material was biblically soft and too vague for Bible study. That is not the case with this current material. It *is* a *relational* Bible study and thus it focuses as much on the people in the group as it focuses on the passage. But there is plenty of content here and, as always with Serendipity, very creative ways of bringing people together.

Discipling Resources
Larry Richards and Norm Wakefield, Zondervan, Grand Rapids, Mich. 1981.

There are currently four studies in this series. They make excellent small group resources. The content is not immense, but neither is the biblical material so vague that it is ignored.

OTHER RESOURCES/ADDRESSES

InterVarsity Press, Box 1400, Downers Grove, IL 60515

NavPress, P.O. Box 6000, Colorado Springs, CO 80934

Serendipity, Box 1012, Littleton, CO 80160

SonPower Youth Sources, 1825 College Ave., Wheaton, IL 60187

Reach Out Ministries, 3117 Majestic Circle, Avondale Estates, GA 30002

1986 Resource Directory for Youth Workers, ed. by Jim Hancock, Zondervan, Grand Rapids, MI 49506

Youth Specialties, 1224 Greenfield Dr., El Cajon, CA 92021